Gender Optics

By

Shalen Lowell

BRILL

SENSE

LEIDEN | BOSTON

All chapters in this book have undergone peer review.

Library of Congress Cataloging-in-Publication Data

Names: Lowell, Shalen, author.
Title: Gender optics / Shalen Lowell.
Description: Leiden ; Boston : Brill Sense, [2021] | Series: Social
  fictions series, 2542-8799 ; volume 37
Identifiers: LCCN 2020043014 (print) | LCCN 2020043015 (ebook) | ISBN
  9789004445758 (hardback) | ISBN 9789004445741 (paperback) | ISBN
  9789004445765 (ebook)
Subjects: LCSH: Gender-nonconforming people--Fiction.
Classification: LCC PS3612.O8877 G46 2021 (print) | LCC PS3612.O8877
  (ebook) | DDC 813/.6--dc23
LC record available at https://lccn.loc.gov/2020043014
LC ebook record available at https://lccn.loc.gov/2020043015

ISSN 2542-8799
ISBN 978-90-04-44574-1 (paperback)
ISBN 978-90-04-44575-8 (hardback)
ISBN 978-90-04-44576-5 (e-book)

ADVANCE PRAISE FOR
GENDER OPTICS

"In *Gender Optics,* Lowell introduces us to Alex, a young, gender non-binary person living in a society where heteronormative and hegemonic definitions of gender are legalized. Through rich descriptions of Alex's thoughts, actions, and experiences, Lowell takes us through the tensions that Alex must navigate of state-sanctioned gender norms and daily micro- and macro-aggressions that force Alex into acts of conformity. Lowell's honest writing style allows us to believe that this could be both wholly fictional and also painfully close to our reality. *Gender Optics* is a must read for those committed to exploring a deeper understanding of gender inclusion through both a personal and academic dialogue."
– Liza Talusan, PhD, Educator and Strategic Partner, LT Coaching and Consulting, LLC

"Although gender dynamics often show up as leitmotifs in fiction, they rarely take center stage. *Gender Optics* offers a refreshing alternative, with the trappings of coming of age filtered through this central lens. In the town of Springfield, author Shalen Lowell builds a world as dystopian as it is quaint – simultaneously a panoptic nightmare worthy of Foucault and a love letter to the New England coastal towns of their own youth. The atmosphere Lowell skillfully creates made me think of reading Lois Lowry's *The Giver* as a child, and shivering at the chilling images of a society stripped of all warmth and individuality despite its bucolic setting. There's a touch of high fantasy here too, if you squint: the great journey into terrible danger by a brave and diverse adventuring party, although I'm not sure Tolkien ever envisioned a daring rescue quite this queer. Yet for all its congruence with classic works depicting the struggles and triumphs of adolescence, *Gender Optics* has plenty to distinguish it. Perhaps most importantly, the whole novel resonates with a kind of charming awkwardness that will readily ring true for anyone remembering their own adolescence. And

Lowell likewise captures the essence of trans and nonbinary life with piercing clarity: terrible trauma shot through with the piercing joy of simple pleasures shared with friends."
– Xan Nowakowski, PhD, Assistant Professor at the Department of Geriatrics and Department of Behavioral Sciences and Social Medicine at FSU College of Medicine

"I loved this novel, and I really want to be friends with Alex! Lowell captures the nuances of gender norms and inequalities in a fascinating manner in *Gender Optics*, and does so with a cunning mixture of realism and speculation sure to thrill readers. *Gender Optics* is not just a story about gender; it is a beautiful journey of friendship, revolution, and ingenuity that will have readers rapidly flipping pages to see what comes next."
– J. E. Sumerau, PhD, author of *Via Chicago* and *America through Transgender Eyes*

"Shalen Lowell's debut novel provides readers with a very contemporary interrogation of the ways in which we enforce small boxes of identity and in the process erase nonbinary and gender nonconforming identities and lives. Reminiscent of the diasporic world of Margaret Atwood's *The Handmaid's Tale*, *Gender Optics* presents us a world just a tiny bit left of our own, in which (inevitable) rightwing sentiment has resulted the criminalization of those who cannot 'perform' within the accepted gender binaries. A genre-defying read that encapsulates the idea of social fiction, this is a book for those who might have wondered why infusing your courses with fiction is such a rich tool for student learning. But if you only think of this as a novel for Gender Studies courses, then you are missing its central point. By providing a rich and complex examination of queer lives, and the ways we police gender, this is a text vital for courses in contemporary history, psychology, business management, sociology, biology, communications, neurology, nursing, health studies, dysto-pian studies and any course that touches on human beings. This is also a novel for everyone providing a desperately needed glimpse into

cisheteronormative hegemonic societies that helps us finally see the entire face of humanity in all its complex shades."
– **U. Melissa Anyiwo, PhD, Professor and Coordinator of Black Studies at Curry College, Massachusetts**

"In their debut novel, Shalen Lowell writes of a dystopian world where gender is regulated by the State. This cautionary tale reflects the subtle (and not so subtle) ways in which our society is preoccupied with the maintenance of a gender binary and of gender norms. *Gender Optics* is a well-written speculation of where legislation such as bathroom bills could lead."
– **Jessica Gullion, PhD, Associate Professor of Sociology at Texas Woman's University**

"Lowell has written a compelling novel that reminds me of a non-binary handmaids' tale. Here is a story that wrestles with the nuances of gender by showing how Alex, who identifies as non-binary, upends polarized thinking about gender to offer us a new model of gender as a person-centric concept. Through Alex, we see the possibility of the what-if: What if we could be seen as we are, as our own person? This novel should be required reading for everyone."
– **Sandra L. Faulkner, PhD, author of *Poetic Inquiry: Craft, Method and Practice***

"*Gender Optics*, true to its title, offers a near-future lens onto our volatile and uncertain present to illuminate how non-binary, genderfluid, and gender-variant people must negotiate the distorting gaze of cisgender-normative, transphobic culture. Complete with dystopian fascist biopolitics in the form of gender-scanners and gender IDs issued by the Foundation for the Protection of Normative Gender, this is a world of Orwellian paranoia, a world of panoptic gazes to be averted, blocked, refused, and subverted – as well as of furtive gazes cast in the hope of being returned in solidarity, empathy, love, and lust. Through the coming-of-age narrative of non-binary, budding intellectual and writer Alex, Lowell offers a chronicle of the fraught

trajectory from self-erasure and shame to self-acceptance and pride in what they provocatively call the 'Hegemonic Hellscape' of enforced gender norms. With keen intelligence, sensitive characterization, and an inspiriting humor, *Gender Optics* connects the personal and the political to tell an intimate story that explodes binarized, cisnormative assumptions. Through the resulting kaleidoscope, Lowell observes love in its many forms: the love between self and other, the love that defines genuine social justice, and the deeply humane empathy that it takes to alter historical structures of exclusion and open up new pathways for entry. Lowell's brisk, imaginative narrative is a valuable contribution to the growing body of LGBTQI literature, deserving of a place on the shelf between Jack Halberstam's *Trans* and Jia Qing Wilson-Yang's *Small Beauty*."
– Jared F. Green, PhD, Stonehill College

"*Gender Optics* presents the reader with a powerful indictment of hegemonic gender roles and of the capitalist consumer economy that exploits them. Part dystopian fiction, part theoretical tract, *Gender Optics* rejects generic boundaries as it presents a clear-eyed assessment of deep-seated cisgender prejudice and a poignant account of the search for a genderfluid and nonbinary self. Deeply compelling and not to be missed."
– Helga Duncan, PhD, English Department, Stonehill College

To Patricia

Your endless love, light, and friendship inspire me more every day

CONTENTS

Acknowledgments   xiii

Academic Introduction   xv

Part 1: Measuring Deviation

Prologue   3

Chapter 1   5

Chapter 2   23

Chapter 3   37

Chapter 4   45

Chapter 5   57

Part 2: Reflections in the Dove Prism

Chapter 6   65

Chapter 7   73

Chapter 8   85

Chapter 9   91

Chapter 10   95

Chapter 11   103

Chapter 12   109

Chapter 13   119

Chapter 14   125

Chapter 15   135

Chapter 16   143

Chapter 17   149

Chapter 18   159

Part 3: The Visible Spectrum

Chapter 19   169

Chapter 20   175

Chapter 21   187

Chapter 22   193

Chapter 23   199

Chapter 24   203

Chapter 25   209

Questions for Class and Book Club Discussions   219

Appendix: Gender Terminology Reference Chart   221

About the Author   223

ACKNOWLEDGMENTS

I have dreamed of publishing a novel since I began writing. So, to finally reach this personal watershed moment is indescribable and fulfilling in a way only other writers can fully understand.

First and foremost, I want to extend a heartfelt thank you to Shea, Patricia Leavy, my parents and family, my closest friends, and my sibling, Rowan. Without your unwavering love, support, and encouragement, this novel would not exist today.

Shea, thank you for being the best hubby, rock, and support system a spouse could ever ask for. You continue to light up my life and support me in my professional and creative endeavors more than I ever thought possible. I hope I do the same for you. I love you more than everything.

To my beta readers, I appreciate you and your detailed and thoughtful feedback more than I say. Thank you for welcoming *Gender Optics* into your lives and hearts.

I also want to extend a warm thanks to Katie Lowery, Jolanda Karada, John Bennett, Els van Egmond, and everyone at Brill | Sense for their dedication to this project and for giving me such a valuable opportunity to express my creativity.

And finally, to all my nonbinary and gender nonconforming friends and chosen family – both those whom I've met and those I have not – you are my greatest inspiration, and your successes are the well from which I draw my own personal strength.

ACADEMIC INTRODUCTION

Picture it: One late summer afternoon in a bookstore café, I was in the midst of penning a chapter on nonbinary and gender nonconforming gender expression, acceptance, and exclusion. Coffee in one hand and my scribbled notes in another, I glanced up from the trenches of my rough introduction and noted a passerby staring point-blank at me, a perplexed expression scrawled across his face. Unfortunately, this wasn't the first time I'd been on the receiving end of a look injected with utter consternation. To wit, that day I had worn my black T-shirt with the word *Genderfluid* plastered across the front, and my first thought was a chilly and uncomfortable one: *Is he trying to clock my gender? Is he thinking, "What gender is that person?"* With still-meager representation of the gender nonconforming spectrum in the media, this moment impressed upon me the feeling of an outlaw, and a writhing paranoia rose from the depths of my belly. I sat with the acute feeling of being targeted, of the realization that at any moment, some bigoted stranger could hurl an insult my way without thinking twice, accusing me of being an abomination by merely existing and trying to live my life.

This discomfort was not new, so I pressed on, a new, nebulous idea for a future novel forming in my mind. Little did that stranger know that from that brief interaction, the initial seeds for *Gender Optics* had been planted.

In both passive and active measures, hegemonic cisheteronormative societies seek to silence and render invisible the people who fall outside these systems' monolithic, binary gender and gender presentation "norms." Just as the sprawling branches of a river delta sink into the surrounding estuary, so too does the normative grasp of binary society sprawl out and entrench itself in countless institutional forces.

The normative gender binary holds dominion over almost everything, whether we choose to realize it or not. From gendered restrooms in restaurants, malls, schools, doctor's offices, and public places, to segregated clothing departments in the same store, to social condemnation of gender variance and expectations of certain "accepted" gendered behaviors, restrictions and microaggressions against variance are everywhere. In my chapter, "Transcending Gender Binarization: The Systematic Policing of Genderfluid Identity and Presentation" in Dr. Patricia Leavy's edited collection *Privilege Through the Looking-Glass*, I wrote,

> Assumptions about one's gender based on presentation reinforce the standards to which that gender should be judged, and therefore, accepted by cisgender onlookers. There presents itself an expectation that your gender presentation should clearly represent the cisnormative representation of that gender, an oppressive force insisting your gender should "match" the presentation of how that gender is perceived. Gender cannot, and should not, be reduced to gender expression. The policing of gender expression, and especially nonbinary genderfluid gender presentation, creates a disruption between an individual's identity and how that identity is perceived. (Lowell, 2017)

It's this aforementioned disruption that causes a rift in perceived identity; strangers may "read" us and deduce our gender based solely on appearance or clothing, when there may be no normative relation between the two. In this situation, strangers distill our clothing into a finite gender presumption.

Interrogating the systems, cultures, and societal forces that establish strict gender binaries – not only for cisgender people, but for trans people, as well – is of paramount importance as civil rights are stripped from the LGBTQ+ community every day. Even for trans, nonbinary, and gender nonconforming people, there's a standard to which others expect us to adhere: we're expected to "look like" some kind of "recognizable" gender; one acceptable option (to strangers) is to present as the "default neutral masculine." These folks only constitute a fraction of the nonbinary community, and yet that one "approved" presentation is an unspoken standard for all, a benchmark to which we will be knowingly held.

This dynamic was another inspiration for *Gender Optics*. As a trans, nonbinary, and genderfluid person, I sought to openly interrogate and deconstruct the perceived presumptions centered around these standards. What if, for example, normative gender standards were legally enforced? What would that look like? How would our institutions inform and enforce these rules and regulations? What would be the consequences of failing to comply with gender expression standards? What if nonbinary gender(s) were legally outlawed? How can we best represent a kaleidoscope of nonbinary identities and expressions (seen in *Gender Optics* through Xavier, Juneau, Kieran, and others)? It's in the midst of this maelstrom that we join Alex, our genderfluid and nonbinary protagonist who, during the thick of their adolescence, must navigate the choppy waters of lust, love, friendship, schooling, loss, and their city's rigid – and perhaps lethal – gender expectations. In this world, Alex must constantly exchange their true self for safety and compliance, a relentless transaction from which they feel they never will escape.

Alex even employs their own forms of creative expression, fiction and poetry, as a means of questioning the normative, binary gender standards to which they are held through metanarrative reflection, demonstrating that perhaps one of the most impactful ways to do so is through creative expression.

Gender Optics will illustrate, interrogate, challenge, and subvert the harmful products of binary hegemonic systems that often seek, both intentionally and unintentionally, to erase nonbinary and gender nonconforming identities and lives, and to push gender variant folks to the fringes of society. We watch as Alex metamorphoses their feelings of shame, knit from a lifetime of internal repression, into pride, and flourish in living with freedom of expression. *Gender Optics* is an honest and raw examination of queer lives, of the people who struggle under the oppressive weight of societal forces as well as those who survive and thrive.

While *Gender Optics* can be read purely for pleasure, it can also be used as supplemental reading for courses in critical theory, gender theory, gender and sexuality studies, LGBTQ studies, intersectionality, and arts-based research.

REFERENCE

Lowell, S. (2017). Transcending gender binarization: The systematic policing of genderfluid identity and expression. In P. Leavy (Ed.), *Privilege through the looking-glass* (pp. 95–102). Rotterdam, The Netherlands: Sense Publishers.

PART 1

MEASURING DEVIATION

PROLOGUE

"We live in a world rife with misinterpretation," wrote Alex, *"and at the core of this friction exists a universal constant, a vehicle fraught with rusty and consistent misfires: language.*

"Simultaneously so definitive and yet so fluid, language and the meaning we inject into every word is slippery, laying the foundation for an exhaustive, critical inner analysis in which we turn word over word to determine whether our own messages were received and interpreting the messages of others.

"The process is relentless.

"Words are tricky. We accept their foretold meaning, the inherent power in that fabricated meaning, and the resulting ramifications on our life as truth until we question that powerful authority.

"'Girl,' for example. Or 'female.' Or 'binary.'"

***

"A parabola is missing its mark here."

"What do you mean, Alex?" Ryan queried, thoroughly stumped.

"You know how parabolas curve according to a predetermined equation? They bend to some sort of rule, a truth?"

"I guess?"

"Well, imagine two axes, x and y, sketched on graph paper. Those axes represent binary gender."

"Okay, where are you going with this?" Ryan persisted.

"I'm the parabola, but no matter how I try to recalculate myself and interrogate my gender, 'girl' doesn't ever feel quite right. Attaching that descriptor to myself feels… uncomfortable, unsettling, uncanny. My parabola's vertex rests on the 0.5 tick mark, and despite its plot adjacent to the binary axes, it's always just shy of settling there. My equation is different than the standard."

Ryan suggested, "Well, if 'girl' doesn't feel right, what about 'demi-girl?'"

"Hmmm, maybe. I may have to try on and exchange gender terms until something feels right. It's hard to explain," Alex despaired. Then, in a moment of panic, they said, "But don't say anything, Ryan. Not a peep, please."

"Not a peep." He smiled.

"I wish I could fast-track this uncertainty. It's painstaking, frustrating, and downright blasphemous."

"You'll get there."

"I hope I live long enough to write about this experience someday," Alex dreamed.

CHAPTER 1

"In theater, gender is performative. That's precisely why Viola, and by extension the actress in her role, is permitted to dress as a man with no repercussions. She disguises herself as a man, and no one is the wiser. No one cares. The audience knows – is supposed to know – that it's all a charade, a mere act. Now, if Viola ever wanted to cease the charade, to call herself at once a man and a woman, or some gender in between, or no gender at all – well then, we'd have a problem on our hands, or so say the conservatives. Heaven forbid. God forbid. Society forbid.

"Society forbids it.

"Really. Fluid gender, nonbinary gender, it's all forbidden here in this purgatory I've named the Hegemonic Hellscape.

"Everyone dresses the same, not because they elect to, but because they absolutely must."

"If only you could get that bit published." Alex felt the soft prickle of Ryan's low, even voice in their ear, and in response, they yanked the composition notebook from his sightline and firmly shut it. Shrugging him off, Alex rolled their eyes and slid the book under their thighs and out of sight, pressed against the charcoal-burnt picnic tabletop. "Oh, the burden of the creative forces, eh?"

"Yeah, yeah, I know how it goes," Alex replied with a resigned sigh. "Not even the black-market press would circulate something this explicit and personal. I'm well aware of that."

Ryan smirked, knowing and devilish. Alex knew Ryan well enough to know that he lit up when he was most mischievous, not that he got much opportunity to exercise that impish tic these days. "Mutiny cloaked in plain sight, huh? Pretty bold of you, my friend."

Alex removed the classic black-and-white composition book from under them, yet another thing that, at first glance, was like the billion others of its kind. "Yup, hiding in plain sight. Unassuming. Completely."

"Like you?" Ryan said.

"Like me."

***

The sun started to dip closer to the city skyline, queuing Alex and Ryan's exit from Springfield's esplanade, five paces from the river that split the city in half. To their right sat the city's infamous half-dome Hatch Shell concert venue, its own shadow stretching out in a long yawn to bathe the pair in a chilly, late summer shade. Dismounting from the picnic table, the pair plodded past the usual Saturday afternoon riptide of familiar strangers who scurried home with their groceries. Arriving at Downtown Crossing, they pivoted toward Ryan's apartment and he stopped, stock-still in the middle of the sidewalk. Alex plowed into him, nearly thrusting him into the street between two idling vans.

"What the... Why..."

"Sorry, sorry, sorry," Ryan apologized, waving his hands in front of him. "My bad, Alex, my bad." He pointed up at the five-story building coming up on their left, the teal neon sign nearly illegible in its branded cursive. "I know how much you loathe shopping, but I just remembered that I promised my mum I would pick up a new pair of slacks for school while we were out."

"Approved by the Foundation for the Protection of Normative Gender?"

"FPNG-approved, indeed."

Alex scoffed. "Ugh, shopping is the worst. I won't even get to hang with you if we go in."

"I'd owe you *big* time. Please? Just pretend you're looking for button-ups and roam the store aimlessly."

"Well, you know I'd love a new button-up, but I can't exactly buy the kind I want here."

Ryan broke out his signature cunning smile and said, "How about this: I owe ya, so I'll buy you one myself. I know your size. If they ask, I'll just say it's a gift. Which it is. They'll never know," he winked.

"Yeah, they certainly won't, since I could never wear a men's shirt in public." The hurt in Alex's voice was as palpable as the shirts displayed on the pale and lifeless mannequins in the store window.

"I know." Ryan sighed. "So, do you want one or not?"

"Duh." Alex flashed the smallest hint of a grin.

Ryan grabbed their hand and led them to the storefront. "You're the best," he said. "And hey, at least it's better than sitting out on the street, pretending to window-shop."

"All I do these days is window-shop."

Ryan offered another sad smile, swiftly kissed them on the hand, and walked toward the men's store entrance. Dejected, Alex slowly headed for the women's.

With little else left to do, Alex let the tide of shoppers carry them into the glass vestibule, only to be halted as they closed in on the gender scanners, which permitted entrance into their gender-assigned side of the store. Alex dutifully removed their Gender ID from their wallet, previously hidden in the pocket of their skirt. As they'd learned in elementary school, only your FPNG-issued identification could permit you entrance into such stores and institutions, any place the organization deemed necessary to be gender-segregated, which were most these days. Driver's licenses and all that jazz were secondary IDs and never sufficed in these instances. Their government-issued and government-approved gender was the ever-present qualifier, Alex had learned. As they waited for their turn at the scanner, they glared with disdain at their picture. Nothing about the stark profile, long curly hair, or shirt buttoned up to the neck (which always reminded Alex of those dolls they were suffocated with as a child) felt representative of who they were as a person. To the right of the picture read the following:

Alexandra V. Cesario
Gender: FEMALE

FEMALE, in all caps. Those "out" trans people who chose to transition were marked with TM (for trans male) or TF (for trans female). As Alex often noted that binary trans people, though relatively accepted by the structures that bound Springfield, and hell, probably the whole country, still received a qualifying "T" on their Gender IDs. Forget flying under the radar. Everything about you, your body, your gender, and your identity, was fair game to be defined. Official markers like these consistently and, more importantly, legally reinforced

7

cisgender stereotyping in a manner with very dire consequences should one identify or desire to present against them.

These sterile entrance vestibules, uniform across every clothing store in the city, sat in stark contrast to the colorful displays outfitted in the store beyond. They resembled the automated turnstiles Alex knew from the subway. To enter, Alex scanned the back of their barcoded Gender ID – *beep*, gender confirmed – then they'd be permitted or denied access to that section of the store based on their credentials. *Impersonal processing at its finest*, thought Alex.

As they approached the turnstiles, Alex glanced sidelong to their right and saw Ryan apace with them, separated by a Plexiglass wall. Looking at him across the way and having their vague reflection projected back at them, Alex couldn't help but imagine how it would feel to enter the store from the other side. Not that the resulting binarization would solve all their quandaries, but still. It would be nice.

With slumped shoulders and a heavy head, Alex scanned their ID and was granted access to the "female-approved" section of the store.

***

Skirts, blouses, bras, pantyhose, headscarves, and hooped jewelry in every size assaulted Alex as they forced themselves into the store. This was a foreign landscape to Alex, but one into which they found themselves forcibly thrown almost every day. On these shopping trips, Alex was reminded, perhaps more visibly than ever in the face of gendered consumerization, that in their society, their city, their world, one does not hide one's gender identity. One can't even mask their gender identity, tucked away amongst a diverse and intersectional set of other identities. In Alex's world, you *were* your gender identity.

They let their fingertips graze a spinning rack of particularly loud and gaudy skirts, comprising every color in the visible spectrum, avoiding the eyes of the other people in the store. *If only mum were here*, Alex wished as they weaved among the constricting, crowded racks and leaving no trace of their winding path behind. *At least she knows how torturous shopping is, even if she can't understand it. Or me. Not completely.*

It seemed like such an infantile wish to Alex, wanting their mum's presence more than anyone else, even above Ryan, who was no doubt shopping happily in his designated section of the clothing store. Shopping without the constant fear of being questioned, discovered, or targeted would be acceptable, a welcome change. Even Alex's dad would be a steady source of comfort, not that he would be permitted in this section. They craved an older adult to guard and defend them, at least when they were alone in public. They longed for the protection of anyone who knew how to navigate these gendered systems more effectively than them, someone who'd been living under this gendered regime for longer than they had.

In that moment, Alex had an epiphany. Who better than themselves to navigate the gender laws and politics of their society? They'd escaped notice of the FPNG so far, hadn't they?

"Alexandra! Alexandra!"

Lost in thought as they were, Alex barely registered someone calling their given name from across the store, someone on their periphery. Whoever Alexandra was should find her friend, mother, aunt, whoever, they thought. The voice was quite interruptive, so much so that they turned to locate the source of the call above the general cacophonous clicks of racks, hangers, and changing curtains. In a dawning moment of dreaded realization, they realized that call must be for them. The last time they heard their birth name was in school two days ago, before the long weekend. *Of course* this person could be addressing them.

Turning on their heel, Alex recognized, to their annoyance and moderate fear, Mrs. Du Bois, their twelfth-grade English Literature teacher, waddling straight toward them from across the store with her eight-year-old daughter in tow and carrying what seemed like fifteen hangers full of clothes. A kind, squat woman with a fire-engine red bob, Mrs. Du Bois was a hoot, and downright entertaining as a teacher. But under her smile and wit, Alex always suspected she was watching them, keeping a close eye on them, sizing them up. Alex would admit that they felt that way about almost anyone who wasn't close friends or family, but the feeling they got from Mrs. Du Bois was slightly more devious. The daughter looked pleasant, if peeved – the expression in her eyes betraying her – as if she and her mother had been at this for hours.

As if to confirm their suspicions, Mrs. Du Bois gave Alex a small pat on the arm and exclaimed, "Ah! What a lovely day to be out shopping, huh? We've been here since just after lunch. Gosh, I just love a sale. Plus, we may as well strike while the iron is hot to restock our fall and winter wardrobes. How are you, dearie?"

Alex had to physically restrain themselves from twitching at the word "dearie," cringing to their core. They also noted, with a sidelong glance outside the shop windows, that the warm afternoon sun and balmy late summer breeze indicated it *was* a lovely day, just not one to be stuck inside shopping. *Torturous.*

Alex forced what they hoped would pass for a casual smile and replied, "Oh fine, thanks! Ryan wanted to go shopping so I decided to tag along. Picture day necessities and all that."

"Ah, how lovely! Are you going to pick up anything for yourself? A new skirt, perhaps? You look so cute today, by the way!"

Alex tried to mask their nervous laughter as bashfulness, brushing back their hair and rubbing the back of their neck to feign embarrassment. Inside, Alex felt as though they were dying, a cold sweat skittering up their back. "Haha! Thanks, Mrs. Du Bois."

"Oh dear, where are my manners? This is my daughter, Anna." Mrs. Du Bois pushed her daughter forward, and Anna offered a small smile and wave, which Alex returned. "Yessiree, I hope she grows up to be as lovely a young lady as you, Alexandra!"

"Oh, I dunno…"

"Oh, please!" Alex had to hand it to her – as normative as their teacher was, she was a decent person. She favored Alex in school, and talked endlessly after class about what a bright future Alex had ahead of them, as a writer or whatever career path they chose. Still, Mrs. Du Bois would not be reading any of the "treasonous" essays Alex often penned in their composition notebook at home, which they kept stuffed under their bed mattress, and Alex wished they could dock a few points from her each time she referred to them as a "young lady." That phrase was definitely Alex's least favorite of all the gendered crap they'd been called over the years. Alex forcibly stifled an eye roll.

With her free hand, Mrs. Du Bois gestured to Alex, as if presenting them to her daughter as the picture of perfect femininity. "Yes, I've said to the English department – off hours, of course. Don't want to be accused of favoritism." She offered a wink. "Anyway, I've told them all that Alexandra is the best girl in my class this year. So bright, intelligent, and responsive. You've got a lot going for you, dearie."

"Well thank you, Mrs. ..."

She waved Alex off mid-sentence. "Nonsense, of course, of course. It's all true. And I'm sure you'll settle down with a lovely man someday, too!"

Alex blushed. Settling down, getting married, that was all shelved in the very back of their mind. They felt they had enough to worry about at the moment – not just normal teenager things like finishing high school and summer jobs and college searches, but also hiding their true gender – to think about anything in the realm of romantic relationships. *Anyway*, Alex thought, *what if I don't want to settle down with a cis man? Cishet folks are often so quick to assume someone's compass of attraction, but the truth often isn't that plain.*

I'm bisexual, and yes, I'm attracted to men, but I'm also attracted to multiple genders, some more than others. Perhaps I walk the bisexual/pansexual line, but bi always felt right to me. Not that I'd tell Mrs. Du Bois any of this. It's none of her business and she could never understand.

"Ha... Yeah..."

"So, are you shopping for anything special?"

"Umm, not really. Just browsing." Alex glanced again at the waning sunlight, silently praying for Ryan to finish as soon as possible. They noticed Mrs. Du Bois following their gaze and added, "I'm all stocked up, just wanted to see if anything struck my fancy; really, I'm just waiting for Ryan to finish his shopping list."

Alex swore that their teacher winked just then, but maybe they were seeing things. Mrs. Du Bois broke out into a huge grin.

"Aww, that's nice, dear. You and Ryan seem very close. What a great relationship."

"Oh, we're not…"

"Not that I'm trying to pry, of course!"

"No, no. Ryan and I are nothing more than steadfast friends, believe me."

"Oh, well that's nice, too." Her wide smile shrunk by a hair or two. Not that Alex thought Ryan wasn't attractive; he was. But just because you're attracted to your friends, doesn't mean you want to date them. At that moment, Alex felt a soft vibration in their skirt pocket. Saved by the buzz. Retrieving their phone, they made their excuses to Mrs. Du Bois ("My mum's checking in, I should take this."), and waved goodbye as they turned toward a rack of particularly fluorescent floral skirts to check their phone. The incoming text was from Ryan:

hey, all done! Waiting outside.

Alex looked up hopefully, and found Ryan waving at them from the sidewalk outside the shop's window. They flashed a brief smirk in his direction and maneuvered an immediate path to the exit, relieved to finally be on the cusp of being able to breathe again.

***

"Did you get the button-up you promised?" Alex had to know that the torture was worth the outcome as they left the shops behind.

"How could I forget?" Ryan brandished his shopping bag of new gender-approved purchases for emphasis.

"Thanks, friend."

"Anytime. See anyone you know?"

"Regretfully, yes," Alex admitted. "Mrs. Du Bois was out shopping with her daughter. Well, probably still is."

"She's not that bad, right?"

Alex pulled their gaze from the many converging cracks in the sidewalk to meet his eyes. In public, they usually kept their eyes far ahead, should they need to sidestep any oncoming pedestrians without making eye contact. "Yeah, she's fine. I mean, she's nice enough; she said a lot of polite gendered things about me as a student."

"So, the usual?"

"Yup. 'She,' 'dear,' 'dearie,' 'cute,' 'young lady.' Ugh, I HATE 'young lady.' I wouldn't expect anything less. She's just so…"

"Cis? Typical?" Ryan fished for the right descriptors.

"Exactly. Cistypical," Alex chuckled. They embraced the humor and let the feminine-coded compliments from their teacher slide. They often tried to find the humor in these moments, if they could. What was the alternative? (Being crushed by the ceaseless weight of living a forcibly gendered life?)

"Speaking of cistypical…" Ryan nodded toward the ubiquitous, government-stamped FPNG agenda poster that graced the façade of Springfield's Medical Center. The flashy lights and window displays of the shopping district, an assault on the senses in their own regard, were behind them. As they walked through the outskirts of the city, Alex recognized that these posters, printed right from every nonbinary person's dystopian nightmare, were vibrantly visible against the increasingly stark, sickly, gray landscape, bold in their entropic flashiness. Despite their mass production, folks like Alex felt emotionally assaulted every time they laid eyes on one. For Ryan, the posters were a fierce and threatening reminder of the binary he had to carefully toe. Although his presentation was decidedly binary, no matter how much time passed, he felt he would never be comfortable within the confines of the (FPNG's rigid gender definitions.)

"What a wicked reminder," Ryan remarked.

"Wicked is putting it mildly," said Alex.

Below the title, ("Presented by the Foundation for the Protection of Normative Gender) (FPNG)," the boilerplate poster featured a stickman and stickwoman, like the ones on binary restroom signs; a thick line separated the sections for Men and Women. The poster's content was printed in formal, serif font, so precise.

Presented by the Foundation for the Protection of Normative Gender (FPNG) The City of Springfield

The FPNG was formed in accordance with our mission to protect and preserve the binaries hitherto established by normative gender and the principles therein. The Gender Guidelines outlined below are policed by the Foundation.

♂ **Men** ♂	♀ **Women** ♀
Terminology	*Terminology*
Biological sex: Male/Trans Male Required Hormonal Makeup: Testosterone Genitals: Penis (Trans men: Synthetic packers required) **Gender ID must reflect M or TM	Biological sex: Female/Trans Female Required Hormonal Makeup: Estrogen Genitals: Vagina (Trans women: Tucking or bottom surgery required) **Gender ID must reflect F or TF
Permitted Masculine Presentation	*Permitted Feminine Presentation*
Short hair (above the ear) Pants/slacks Legged shorts No more than five pieces of jewelry worn at any time No makeup T-shirts permitted	Long hair (below the ear) Skirts Legged pants (ONLY if a skirt is worn over them) Jewelry unlimited Conservative makeup encouraged T-shirts permitted

Forbidden	*Forbidden*
Skirts, kilts, skorts, or any apparel of that nature Long hair (below the ear)	Legged pants or shorts worn without a skirt Short hair (above the shoulder)

Strictly Prohibited

Genders and presentations not included above are strictly prohibited.

In accordance with the law, failure to comply with these guidelines will result in immediate removal from the city and mandated rehabilitation.

First-time offenders will receive a fine in lieu of removal if the offenses are amended within five (5) days and accompanied by a completed contract, signed by five (5) friends or family members.

Second-time offenders will be transported from Springfield to one of the regional Panoptica.

No exceptions.

Transgender individuals who willingly comply with the above FPNG guidelines will be protected by the full authority of the Foundation. Trans women and trans men must abide by the above as fully as their cisgender counterparts.

For information regarding medical transition from your gender assigned at birth, please contact the Springfield Medical Center, as well as your healthcare provider for coverage. For renewals or alterations of your Gender ID, please visit the Springfield FPNG headquarters or any of our regional offices.

For further details, guiding principles, and gender facts, please visit https://fpng.gov

"Got to love the end part, right?" Alex said with a sting of sarcasm and bitterness.

"Absolutely, it's my favorite part."

"Fabricating binaries on top of binaries, just to make you work in their system."

"Yup."

"True ingenuity. FPNG really knows how to strike fear in the hearts of even those who comply with these ridiculous standards."

"Yeah, I imagine that even most cisgender people, despite their never-ending privilege, still get wary when glancing over one of these things."

"You mean gender nonconforming folks, too?"

"Yeah. The FPNG, by very definition, targets both nonbinary and gender nonconforming folks, and GNC people are not immune from the hellfire of the Foundation. Right?"

"Definitely," confirmed Alex. "Depending on the context, GNC people might not feel as threatened if they are also cis, but there is an overlap between those who identify as nonbinary *and* GNC.

"Not that I'm the end-all-be-all authority, but to me, nonbinary means that an individual does not identify solely as male, female, or any other concrete binary gender identity. That's definitely not the case for all nonbinary people, but that's the best off-the-cuff explanation I have. And to me, gender nonconformity is this wider bucket of gender variance; GNC folks may exhibit behavior or gender expression that does not align with gender norms. Being nonbinary does not always mean you are gender nonconforming, and vice versa. And nonbinary is not mutually exclusive with being androgynous."

"That's a pretty apt description."

"Either way, cis or not, if you don't comply with their guidelines, yer out," Alex said, shooting their thumb over their shoulder. "I'd wager that us nonbinary folks have it the hardest. I'm not out, I'm not binary trans, so I get the feeling I'm being watched at every turn. Do you ever feel like that? As someone who has transitioned?"

Ryan sighed. "I do. I hate that I do. Like many other binary trans people in this city, I imagine that once you transition to 'the other binary,' as they've categorized it, you're marked. You're on their 'must watch' list. My body aligns with my gender more than ever, but I imagine the FPNG must be thinking, *What if Ryan was lying?* Obviously, that argument is bull crap, not to mention that we already are our own genders. They just don't see that."

"For sure. I just wish I didn't have to be ashamed of who I am, of being a genderfluid, transgender person. I'd love more emotional support, but that's not going to happen without exposing myself to new dangers. I have to tread so carefully with new friends."

"And they own our bodies. They own my body. It's written there in black and white. Our biology, gender, sex, whatever – it's all regulated. We're regulated."

"Ryan, it's rhetoric like this that makes me question why you insist on stopping at these things every chance you get. We already know what they say."

"I have to keep my eyes open for updates, new rules to follow."

"They'd broadcast a citywide alert if they amended the rules."

"That may be true, but…"

"But what?" *Why would Ryan want to gawk at these damn posters? They bore into me like watchful eyes, making me feel under suspicion. Targeted.*

"But… I guess I just have some morbid fascination."

"With the imminent demise of all nonbinary and gender nonconforming people?"

Ryan avoided Alex's eyes, turning so they couldn't detect the downcast look on his face. "Don't we know it…"

"I'm sorry, I didn't mean to sound so blasé. You know that I fear for my life as much as any other nonbinary person in this damn city."

"I know." Ryan was clearly hurt.

Placing their hand on one of his shoulders, Alex offered the only sense of comfort they could conjure in this hellscape, knowing all too well about whom he was thinking in these moments of defeat. "I miss Juneau, too."

"I wonder where she is."

"We know exactly where she is, where *they* took her. It doesn't help, but maybe the knowledge is enough."

CHAPTER 1

"What do you suppose they're doing with her?"

"Ryan, I don't know what they're doing. I don't think I want to know. What do they do to the people they 'remove and reform?' I've made up my mind: I'd rather not know. It would torture me day and night to think of Juneau like that, imprisoned."

Ryan's ten-thousand-yard stare revealed his lack of presence in the moment. For the first time in the four months since Juneau's disappearance, Alex witnessed the full gravity of Ryan's loss, of *their* loss. They lost their closest friend because Springfield deemed her a threat to society. Alex's was tormented by wondering: wondering if Juneau was safe, wondering which Panoptic she'd been sent to, wondering how she'd been caught, and wondering if they'd ever be arrested, too. Juneau and Alex, they'd been nonbinary kin, after all, having met through Ryan at an underground youth group he attended. The turnstile of worries and questions were endless.

Soon after their meeting, Ryan had fallen in love with Juneau.

Finally working up the strength to pull himself back into their present conversation, he continued, "Call it my morbid fascination again, or a teenage longing or whatever, but I want to know. Conversion therapy? Religious reform akin to what happens in the worst parts of the Bible Belt?"

"Ryan, can you stop? I can't imagine… I don't want to."

"Okay, okay, I'll stop. I'm done for the day, let's go." Alex's fingers creeped down Ryan's arm, finally finding his warm hand. Linking their hands together, they walked headlong into the sunset.

***

Some folks conceptualize genderfluidity as a sliding scale, like a finite line graph capped with a pole at each end. For them, one pole represents the binary male gender and the other is the binary female gender. In this view, gender can shift and is fluid, but is always polarized in relation to one of those two options. Gender is always relative to those metropoles, some believe; one is either more or less female or more or less male.

But that illustration of genderfluidity is too rigid a structure for me. I see genderfluidity as a person-centric concept, where the individual is the singular pole around which all gender possibilities revolve; they're at the center of a kaleidoscopic spiderweb, in which each intersection of overlapping webbing is one location on the gender spectrum as defined by that individual. My gender could be at any given intersection at any given time, or even at multiple intersections or all of them or none at all. There are infinite possibilities for me.

That's not how every genderfluid person illustrates their identity, but for me, gender isn't as defined or rigid as the FPNG or normative folk insist, or even as that sliding scale would illustrate.

As they watched the sun slide further down the slippery slope of Springfield's skyline, Alex made a mental note to journal their thoughts on gender later that night, in the relative safety of their own bedroom. They donned their amber-lensed, tortoiseshell sunglasses for the last leg of their journey home. After escorting Ryan to his family's apartment, far closer to the city center than Alex and their family resided, Alex's pace quickened when they remembered the contraband in their left hand: the button-up Ryan bought them, disguised in a plain, brown paper shopping bag. *Shit.* They tried to play it cool, but each passerby was another potential witness, another opportunity to draw suspicion and unwanted attention. They set their sunglasses firmly in front of their eyes to hide their panic and to counter the sun's burning path down the silver-and-shadow checkerboarded building faces. The sunshine lit a path at Alex's feet, illuminating the way home to relative safety. The autumn season fell palpably upon them and they craved the feeling of thriving in that burnt-orange autumn glory.

Despite their brief nostalgic detour, Alex recognized an inevitability: dinnertime. One subway ride later plopped them on the eastern end of the city, over the Springfield Memorial Bridge. Taking one last look at the river that wound through and bisected Springfield, they hiked up three flights of stairs and arrived at their family's home. Beyond their faded green door with the plastic, gilded number 10 was not a posh, luxury loft, like you'd find at the city center, but to Alex, it was home. It was enough. It was a space in which Alex could hide themselves, sheltered from the world at the end of the day, if but for a short time. It was a place where they could just *be*.

"Welcome home, Alexandra!" Alex's mum chirped upon their entry, but the second their name escaped her mouth in full, she deflated at her mistake, "Sorry. Alex. Welcome home, *Alex*." Recovering on the spot, she ushered her child inside. "How was your day, honey? How's Ryan?"

"Oh, Ryan's good, the same as ever, I guess. We went shopping." Alex gave their mum a knowing look, which their mum returned. She knew they hated shopping.

"Is he coming by for dinner?"

"Nah, he mentioned something about family plans."

"Aww, that's too bad," their mum said. "He's such a sweet boy."

"He is."

Alex's mum drew her face into a sly, coy smile. "Are you sure that you two…?"

Laughing at her transparent insinuation, Alex replied, "Ha, no way mum. You know that." Unlike their probing teachers and classmates, Alex knew their mum meant no harm by the question. *I think she just expects me to settle down with someone, someday.*

"You know we don't care who you end up with, we'll support you no matter what, both of us. But you and Ryan are adorable."

"Ha, thanks mum."

Clapping her hands together to suggest a heavy pivot in the conversation, their mum asked, "Anyway, what did you get?" Alex eyed the bag with a low, guilty glance. "What?" their mum asked.

"Well…" Alex said nervously. *Time to give up the ghost.* "Ryan got me something, actually."

"Oh, yeah?"

"Well, obviously, we can't shop in tandem, so I twiddled my thumbs in the women's department and he picked something up for me in the men's."

"How lovely! Can I see?"

Alex shrugged. "Sure, mum." They unwrapped the orange and black plaid button-up shirt; at first glance, it looked like so many others bought and sold in the women's department, but having been forcibly dressed in many of those, Alex could tell the differences. The straight, non-princess cut sides stood out to their eye. Sure, they could buy button-ups in their permitted section, but not many were sold like this one, and even the straightest cuts were designated "feminine" with gems, trim, frill, or embellishments. They were horrid and unseemly, in Alex's opinion.

Mum gave a nod of approval and a long smile. "Well, why don't you run to your room and put it on for dinner? Your father and Josephine should be along shortly. That'd be nice. Would you like that?"

"Definitely. Thanks, mum."

Plodding across the pristine living room, Alex shut their bedroom door against the world, relishing moments like these, moments of reprieve and solitude. *It's easier to just be me when no one is around*, they thought. *Even with Ryan, when we're in public, I have to pretend.*

Alex peeled their clothes from their skin, warm and aglow from Springfield's summer sun, so unforgiving some days and welcoming on others.

Welcome. I wonder how it would feel to have my gender welcome here, not only welcome when it's stashed away from the public's prying eyes. I would be snatched in a second.

Taking their time, Alex slowly unlocked and opened both of the bedroom's wide, shuttered windows. If they closed their eyes, they could smell a hint of the salted sea air, drifting in from the beaches of the river that wound its way around their city, a tight, restrictive coil which separated the posh residents downtown from those left on the outskirts. Transfixed, Alex drank in the scent as it wove its way into their room on the back of the humid evening wind, held together with the unmistakable bond of petrichor. It was at once thick and sweet and savory – an ideal convergence.

Senses heightened and sanity somewhat restored, they looked into the mirror that was fastened to the back of their door and arranged in front of their rainbow Pride flag. Their body, their genderfluid body, their wonderful, valid, trans nonbinary body flung its reflection

21

back at them. Subtracting their gender-policed clothing relieved and revealed Alex. As this body lay in front of them, Alex marveled for a moment in its splendor, splendor only evident when all clothing was shed, when nothing was expected of them. Their breasts, their slightly stocky shoulders, and their privates were all perfect and valid in their eyes, as well as the eyes of trusted friends like Juneau and Ryan, and maybe even some closeted classmates they didn't know about, as uncomfortable as it was to admit. Validation from strangers, from Springfield's government, from the world was what Alex craved most. Validation and perhaps the ability to change certain areas and processes that came part and parcel with their body – their hips, their period – without having to change everything. *If I'm not a man and I'm not a woman, what am I?*

Who am I?

CHAPTER 2

Lounging on the screened-in porch of their grandmother's summer beach house; watching the wind coax the midday clouds across the shifty sun; relishing the salty, pure, organic ocean breeze, unencumbered by the scent of the city – this was heaven to Alex. In complement to their near-transcendent state were the navy swim trunks they wore and their men's muscle tank that read, "YB EST. 1659," in bold, black letters. Alex savored this freedom for as long as they dared, temporary and sheltered though it may be.

Pen in hand and poised to continue writing, they drank in the forceful rushes of wind that sang their way through the porch screens. Closing their eyes and waiting for the next wake of air, it struck Alex how the wind here sounded like the pounding ocean less than two miles down the road: the soft aftermath of the rustling of leaves signaling the next wave was about to break, the rush of that wind through the lush deciduous trees around them, much like the beach waves curling over the nearby coastline. The rattling of Springfield's trees couldn't hold a candle to the sound of the ocean created by a thick wind drawing its fingers through a full-bodied forest near the coast.

Just five minutes down the road, the town of York boasted a robust LGBTQ culture, and hosted several events that Alex frequented with Josephine, or Jo, as she preferred to be called. They loved the little town, its center packed with yummy restaurants, a piano bar, and a queer club, and its miles of pristine beaches; nevertheless, Alex always felt a tad unsettled. They felt they were allowed to express themselves, but only in the *right* way. Ideally, they'd desire a freer and more accepting space, since they could only be queer in "approved" ways. Thus, when meeting new people at York's cafés and restaurants, Alex only ever revealed that they were bisexual, not a hint more.

"You know, when we head into town later, you can't dress like that," Alex's mum practically admonished, unintentionally reminding them of their place in this world.

Alex shut their eyes, taking a deep breath to temper their reaction. "Yes, I know mum."

"Just let her – sorry, them – have fun while they can," Alex's dad chimed in. He was lounging on the old, metal-framed couch with faded floral cushions, and reading *The Birds* by Daphne du Maurier. The two things that united Alex's family were film and fiction.

"I'm just saying, you and I both know that Alex needs to be careful."

"They know that, duh," added Jo, Alex's younger sibling by two years, her Sudoku book in hand.

The best word Alex could imagine to describe their sister was spritely. Jo was bright, and she was the most optimistic yet practical person Alex knew. She was a beautiful person, yes, but she also possessed the supreme power of making you feel like you mattered, that the universe, and she, loved you just as you were. She was genuine and beautiful and gay, and also, quite badass: she held a black belt in Shotokan karate.

When Alex presented in feminine clothing, people often said that Alex and Jo could be twins, except that Jo's hair was the bright, strawberry blonde counterpart to Alex's own auburn locks. Their eyes, both shades of hazel green, even complemented one another.

Jo plopped down next to Alex and scooped up their long hair into a beanie, which Alex had been struggling with a moment before.

"Thanks, Jo. How's Charlie?"

"She's great!" she said, flashing an inescapably goofy grin. "She's away with her folks in the mountains this weekend. I'd sure love for her to come along with us sometime," Jo said with a pointed glance at both of their parents.

Alex's mum and dad exchanged a cute smirk. "We'll see," their father finally answered.

Before they knew it, Jo shoved her phone into Alex's face and assaulted them with a flood of new selfies that Jo and Charlie had taken together. Alex loved how much they loved each other. For now, it had the flavor of high school romance, but Charlie and Jo's relationship nonetheless gave them hope for a relationship. *One day, when I'm ready.*

"How's the story progressing, Alex?" Jo blurted without thinking. *Oh shit.* She realized her mistake and clapped her hand over her mouth.

Both of their parents looked up, attentive and curious. "You're writing a story?" their mum asked, instantly disinterested in her newspaper word puzzle.

"Oh, yep." Not sure of what to say, Alex thought back to that day by Springfield's waterfront, hiding their notebook from Ryan, from the world.

"What kind?" their mum pushed.

Alex replied vaguely, "Oh, uh, fiction. It's a little autobiographical, but mostly fiction."

"It better not be *too* autobiographical, if you know what I mean." She said it playfully, but Alex was wounded.

Sweat crystallized on Alex's forehead. They ignored it and forged ahead into a straight-up lie. "No, no, nothing to worry about. It's quite proper, I assure you."

Alex thought their parents looked completely unconvinced, but they dropped the issue. *I hope they know I'm smart enough not to share it with those who don't know. Ryan's the only one who's seen it, and even he only caught a glimpse of some stray passages.*

Jo nodded her head in the direction of the door and abandoned her half-finished Sudoku on the worn, floral bench. "Why don't we go for a walk, hmmm?" she asked, gesturing her hand out to Alex.

"Why, that might be nice," Alex's mum chirped.

"We'll be back before dinner in town," Jo insisted as she wrenched Alex from their fretting.

Fleeing the scene of their ersatz interrogation, Alex took the lead and brushed their way through the tall, wild grass that winged the small cape homestead, an outpost for vacation and family time since Alex could remember. They looped around the house and cut down to the petite harbor inlet that they could see from both the open-air back porch and the house's living room, trotting across several other property lines to do so.

Squatting in the harbor were several old dinghies and smaller vessels that were starting to lean sideways as the tide drew itself from the harbor and out to the ocean. Noting this, Alex said, "We should drop by the beach after supper. Looks like the tide is rolling out."

"Yeah, absolutely. Smells like it, too," Jo remarked as she sniffed out the sulfurous hint of low tide.

"Are we putting our feet in the water?"

"Let's save it for later. Plus, let's be honest: even if we dangle our legs off the pier, we're so short, our toes won't reach the water!"

Alex laughed. "I have to admit, you're right. You've got nothing on my five feet, two inches!"

"Puh-lease, you're only two inches taller than me!"

"Okay, okay."

Settling onto the rough wooden dock, Alex took a deep breath and relaxed back into their calm vacation demeanor. As Jo often reminded them, Vacation Alex was quite different than City Alex, less high-strung and jumpy, they'd like to think. It was little wonder why, considering the strictures they could temporarily shed while they were hidden away in a different state.

"Enjoying your vacation?" they asked Jo.

"You know it! I love it up here, summer nostalgia and all."

"Even if you have to tear yourself from Charlie to spend time with little ol' me?"

"Pshhhh, not little ol' you," Jo insisted. "You're my sibling, and as much as this is a rarity for other families, I actually *want* to spend time with you."

"Aww, shucks. I assume you'll have Charlie around for quite a while?"

"If I can manage it!"

"Good, because she's lovely."

Jo's furious blush betrayed her. She smiled, embracing the embarrassing amount that she loved her girlfriend. "You look like you're enjoying this."

"I am, I can't even deny it. I love embarrassing you." Alex's grin widened both at their comment and at the realization that they had two more days in this heaven. "I feel like most teens dread family vacations, but I relish them. I don't want to spend my glory years stuck with my cisnormative peers."

Alex saw Jo shift herself on the edge of the dock, adopting a rare, serious demeanor. Alex was just about to ask her what was wrong when Jo spoke up. "I hope you'll meet someone. Sooner rather than later. I worry about you."

Oh man, that's all. "Ha, for a second there I thought you were going to say something serious! I was concerned."

"I am serious."

Alex waved their sister off. "I know you are. I swear I'm not discounting you. It'll be fine. Plus, I have more pressing concerns on my mind."

"About your senior year?" Jo guessed.

"No, trying to stay alive, to ensure my mental health isn't complete shit, and to avoid getting arrested – you know, normal, average, everyday high school teenager stuff.

"Oh, right. Sorry." Jo rubbed the back of her neck guiltily as an embarrassed flush consumed her face. "Sometimes, I just…"

"Forget?"

"Yeah. I guess I get wrapped up in the normalcy of this," gesturing at Alex's current clothing, "and I forget what you go back to: the repression of your true identity and being forced to assimilate in a gendered costume. I'm sorry."

"S'okay. I wish I could say I'm used to it, but to be perfectly honest, leaving here gets harder each time."

"Maybe someday you'll be able to be yourself?"

"I wish. Not likely in a society where cisnormativity is the only currency."

***

Hours later, Alex followed the maître d' to the last balcony table in the Sand Dollar Restaurant, perhaps the best seat in the house, and plopped down across from their parents.

"The maître d' said this table is usually taken. The view is incredible!" remarked Alex's mum.

"Guess we got lucky. I'll take it!" Jo proceeded to flip through her menu and ponder her options.

"Well, *I* already know what I want," Alex's mum announced and refolded her laminated menu. "I've been looking online all day. Yelp reviewers claim this place has some of the best seafood in town, so baked stuffed lobster it is. I'm surprised we haven't been here before."

"Maybe I'll just get a bowl of the house chowder and a salad."

"Oh, for Pete's sakes, Don," their mum admonished. "We're on vacation!"

"I'm torn between the plank salmon and the fra diavolo pasta," Jo said.

Alex teased, "Yeah, we all know how you like it spicy," giving an exaggerated wink before they opened their menu and scanned its bountiful, if somewhat pricey, options.

Ignoring their growling stomach, Alex allowed their family's chatter to dissolve into background noise as they sized up their surroundings: To their right was the closest beach, no more than half a mile long, early evening fog hugging the houses situated on each end of the unassuming harbor. The deliciously salty ocean spray drifted toward Alex on the wind, and it smelled slightly of seaweed. Those smells together, the ocean and the seaweed, both sun-beaten from the day, were toxic in their addiction, conjuring vivid recollections of many childhood summers spent in the bustling town.

Past the other restaurant goers, wait staff, and bussers, Alex honed in on the Ferris wheel, which framed the entirety of the quaint downtown area, sparkly bulbs running in concentric circles around its outer frame. A crew of motorcycles gunned their engines as they wove through the packed downtown stretch of Railroad Avenue, lined with ice cream and slush vendors, burrito shops, tourist traps, the combination distillery and kettle popcorn store, a sunglasses kiosk, and a small convenience store featuring generic vacation T-shirts for half the price of the store near the zoo. Alex loved it. It resembled so many other small, coastal vacation towns, and yet all the rest were unlike this.

The band of motorcycles directed Alex's sights to the Ferris wheel once again, a main attraction at the end of the shops, as they followed the road's curve.

Vance Joy's voice found Alex's ears from the sound system, the acoustics plucking at their attention with his song "Bonnie and Clyde."

"So, what did you decide on, Alex?"

"Huh?"

"For food? What were you thinking about?" Alex's eyes refocused to find Jo waving her hand in front of their face, hailing them back into the conversation.

Alex realized that their family was staring at them, kindly, but pointed and curious. They felt a chill run down their back, unrelated to the ocean breeze, and it took them a moment to understand their reaction. *That's the same look I get from some strangers.* Alex gulped. *If given a moment of pause, I feel like others see through my carefully constructed costume.*

I'm safe here, Alex reminded themselves. *I'm safe here.*

***

Alex was far from accustomed to gawking at the appearances of strangers, but they'd already gawked for a full minute at how hot this particular stranger was. This person was insanely attractive in profile, with their fiery, electric-blue, curly hair highlighting their crisp features. *The hottest part of any flame is the blue part, isn't it?* Alex thought stupidly, then silently admonished themselves.

Fleeing from their mum, dad, and Jo after dinner for some alone time and a stroll along the sand (Jo wanted to read at the house, anyway), Alex mindlessly meandered until they found themselves at the amusement park abutting the turn at the end of Railroad Avenue. In the midst of the excited park crowd, full to the brim with teenagers and a few young families heading out to a late dinner, Alex found themselves staring at an unusually attractive stranger. They found many kinds of people attractive, but this one? Wow.

Whoever they were, they stood a hundred feet away, manning the "Throw the Dart, Pop the Balloon, Get a Prize" game stand. They seemed rather bored, picking at their nails and waiting for the next guest to try their hand at winning a huge, stuffed, magenta and lime-green dinosaur. Alex wished they could have said that their feet moved toward that booth with a mind of their own, but after a moment of consideration, they told themselves they'd wanted to have a go at a game anyway and they walked toward the attractive – *Handsome? Beautiful? Both?* – stranger.

Something about the person's expression gave Alex pause. They possessed a certain kind of knowing look that disarmed Alex and made them nervous, but they could have just as easily mistook it for the knowing look a carnival worker gives you as you're walking by, tempting you, egging you on to spend your loose dollars on a game of chance or skill.

"Hey, want to play?" the stranger asked as Alex approached.

"Hmmm, maybe. I'm never any good at these things, but I was thinking about it."

Alex sized up this person's publicly presented gender as "male," based on their outward appearance and their lack of makeup and jewelry. Gender deviants tended to keep to the shadows and refrained from expressing their true selves in public. *But why am I attempting to size up this person's gender, anyway? Who am I to presume, of all people?*

In the moment that Alex was consumed with these brief thoughts, the mysterious stranger took the chance to ask, "What's your name?"

They were caught off-guard. *Does he think I'm shy?* "Alex... uh, Alexandra. Yeah. How about you?" *Jesus, why did I stutter?*

"I'm Kieran!"

Alex nodded in approval. "That's a cool name. I always thought mine was pretty bland."

Kieran shrugged. "It seems like an adaptable enough name to me," he said.

"What do you mean by that?"

Waving them off, Kieran replied, "Never mind, never mind."

Alex offered a confused smirk and said the next thing that popped into their head. "I like your septum piercing. When did you get it?"

"The day after I turned eighteen. Parents were too strict, so I waited until I was out of the house to go for it. My dad said to my mom, 'He looks like a bull with that ring in his nose,' but it doesn't matter too much. It's my decision."

"Definitely. I've been thinking of getting one myself, after graduation."

"Septum?"

"No, eyebrow. Less cartilage there, so it might heal faster. That's what I'm thinking, anyway."

Kieran tipped up his head to emphasize the location of the theoretical piercing. "You'd be surprised; the healing wasn't so bad. If I could, I'd get a face full of piercings. My ears, too."

Momentarily ignoring the standards policed as FPNG-approved "male" appearances, Alex said, "Yeah! That would be sick."

"It's too bad, though, with the FPNG's restrictions. You could conceivably get as many as you'd like."

"That's true enough."

Kieran called another employee over, presumably to relieve him of his post, then turned back to Alex. "Hey, I'm off for the night in a sec. Want to walk around?"

"Yeah, that would be cool. I'm not here with anyone."

"By yourself?"

"Yeah, sometimes I like doing these things alone. But I'd like your company." A definitive flush filled Alex's cheeks, which they were sure Kieran noticed. "Uh, if you want to."

As Kieran hopped over the low counter to his booth, using just one arm to support him, Alex couldn't help but give his body a once-over. When he turned to thank his coworker and say goodbye for the night, Alex noticed he had a very toned butt.

Stop it, control yourself. You don't even know this guy.

Kieran turned and touched Alex's freckled and sun-kissed arm, asking, "Ready to go?" Normally, Alex flinched at the unwanted touch of a stranger, but for this guy, right now, Alex decided it was okay, and granted him a silent acceptance.

After they nodded, Kieran suggested, "How about I show you around the place? I grew up one town over, so I could give you the grand tour of downtown."

Alex couldn't help but laugh as they replied, "Thanks! I've actually been up here almost every summer since I was born. I know the ins and outs of York."

"Well, look at you, hot shot."

Alex and Kieran exited the amusement park, now swollen with raucous throngs of teenagers, and headed for the small pizza joint around the block. While many of the other late dinner-goers opted for indoor seating, the pair sat themselves on the makeshift patio that served as the outdoor dining space and ordered meat and veggie pizzas, sans olives.

"So," Kieran started, ripping into his first piece of quattro stagioni pizza, "You been to this place before? It looks a little too rough around the edges for the highbrow folks that vacation here, but it works for us laymen, or should I say, laypeople."

"Yeah, my sister and I actually came here for lunch yesterday."

"Oh, yeah? I'm surprised I didn't see you. I usually come for lunch while I'm working at the park."

"Fancy that." Alex gave Kieran their most highbrow, curious expression while sipping water with their pinky up.

Jittery butterflies filled Alex's stomach when Kieran winked in response, and their entire body felt warm and flush. "Well, have you been to Fisherman's Wharf, just by the highway?"

"Yup, check."

"And certainly, you've been to both of the main beaches?"

"Of course."

"Of course." Kieran trailed off, an impish grin marking his face. "How about Kennebunk Cove?"

"With the drawbridge, where the smaller boats and yachts dock?"

"You've heard of it."

"Yeah, I've been there."

Alex found Kieran's best attempt at frustration to be adorable as hell, sarcastic and laughably coy.

"All right, smart stuff," he said. "I wave the white flag. I'm trying to wow you with my local knowledge, but you're shooting me down."

Rushing to swallow their bite of pizza in time to respond, Alex said, "I can't help it! I told you I've been coming here my whole life."

"That's true. I admit defeat. I just wonder why I haven't seen you before."

"Who knows?"

"Who knows, indeed. Since you know so much about this place already, why don't you tell me a little more about yourself?"

"Well, you know my name. I'm from a city about two states away: Springfield, the metropole of the east, some call it. I live there in an apartment with my mum, dad, and sister, Jo. Hmm, let's see. I just started senior year. I like to write."

He jumped in. "You write?"

"Uh, yeah. Mostly fiction, but I dabble in poetry on occasion."

"What kind of fiction?"

"Fantasy."

Kieran nodded his head in approval. "I'm an artist, myself."

The admission piqued Alex's curiosity, and they asked, "Do you consider writing a form of art?"

"Absolutely. It's a different and spectacular kind of visual art."

"Cool." Alex liked Kieran more than they expected. Over their dead body, however, would Kieran be allowed to read anything they wrote. "So, what kind of art do you practice?"

"Mostly photography, but some painting."

"What do you like to paint?"

"My favorite photographic subjects are people, but I love painting landscapes."

"I've always admired people who can paint. It's mesmerizing to watch. My friend Ryan paints. Well, he takes art classes in school, but he's very talented."

"He sounds like a cool dude. Not to assume, but is he a *friend* friend, or…"

Alex let out an involuntary cackle. "Oh man, why do people always assume that just because Ryan is a guy that there is romantic or sexual interest there? Cracks me up every time."

Kieran put his hands up in defense and said, "Sorry, sorry. It was a dumb question. It was very hetero of me to ask that, I guess. I'm sorry, Alexandra."

Alex hoped their instinctive inner cringe didn't manifest itself on their face just then. Kieran had avoided calling them by their birth name until now, and Alex had hoped to avoid it altogether.

Kieran took an audible breath and nervously asked, "So, you're not seeing anyone, then? No love interests?"

Alex's gaze shot up just as Kieran's eyes plummeted to avoid theirs. "Uh, umm, I wouldn't say that. Not right now, I guess. I think. Are you?"

"Seeing someone? No, but I would like to be. Theoretically, that is." Hearing Kieran's nervous laughter stung Alex with rare, bittersweet hope. *He couldn't possibly be suggesting...?* Alex didn't consider themselves attractive as they were currently dressed, presenting as "FPNG-approved female." They weren't comfortable wearing these clothes; how could they possibly be attractive to anyone else in them? Alex couldn't conceive of the possibility. Would Kieran reject them if he saw them in a more authentic presentation?

***

It was just a kiss, nothing more and nothing less. Alex fully recognized the reality of the situation: they were just two strangers, they had just met, perhaps mere passing or tertiary characters in each other's lives. Alex liked knowing almost nothing about Kieran, and they saw little wrong with manifesting this moment of attraction, right then and there, no strings attached. Their mind felt clear for the first time in memory, as if this moment were meant to be as it is. Nothing more, nothing less. The moment simply *was*, a brilliant simplicity. Whether this clarity was the result of the kiss or the crisp, refreshing breeze rushing through their hair as they spun lazily around the Ferris wheel, they did not know.

All was calm.

Alex broke from the embrace just as their cart reached the top of the Ferris wheel, looking out over the deepening cerulean-blue skyline, a single cloud over the lighthouse out to sea. Then, the two cascaded back to earth, wind still whooshing and heads still abuzz.

The Ferris wheel hitched halfway down its third rotation, jerking Alex and Kieran into one another as the other riders disembarked in pairs. As Kieran turned toward Alex, so did they, slowly closing the gap between their noses and stroking a strong kiss across Kieran's lips. Alex relished the warmth of their face, this momentary happiness and passion both so palatable and savory. They'd never felt anything like it before. Sure, there had been other kisses, but this kiss was a singularity. Kieran's kiss rejuvenated Alex's entire body, and the sensation rested below their belt in a deep attraction altogether new.

"I don't know if this will make a lick of sense to you, Alex," Kieran interrupted, breaking the kiss once more, "But I'm going to say it anyway."

"Hmmm?" Alex failed to wipe the goofy grin from their face, still intoxicated.

"I feel like I see you the way you want to be seen, not as everyone else sees you."

"Oh, yeah? How's that? You barely know me. We just met."

"I know, but when I look at you... I can't explain it. Somehow, I see you the way I think you want to be seen, clothes, hair, dress, style, what have you. I see you as your person. As you are."

Upon hearing, "As you are," a cold sweat worked its way down Alex's back. *What could he know? How could he know?*

"I don't know what you mean..." *Could I be overthinking what he seems to be implying? It couldn't be. No one's that good...*

Kieran's eyes glinted with the reflection of the nearby carousel as their cart passed it, edging to the ground in its final descent, and he wrung his hands nervously. "I can't explain it, but I feel safe telling you this. I'm only presenting as..."

Ka-chunk. The Ferris wheel operator threw up the bar holding Alex and Kieran in place. "Hope ya enjoyed your ride!" she smiled.

Alex often felt like they endured life in a series of hitches, jolt after jolt, and this experience was just another of many.

As the pair dismounted, Alex reflexively took Kieran's hand in theirs, and Kieran asked, "Will I be seeing you again?"

Both ambivalent and scared, scared of what Kieran would ask next and equally scared of what they might say in response, Alex replied, "I don't know."

"Why not?"

"You know I live in the city." Alex mustered the courage to look at Kieran head-on. "I'm honestly not sure when we'll be back up here. School's back in session. Maybe in October?" They floundered for some reasonable explanation that didn't sound like a pathetic cop-out. Every fiber of Alex's body told them to run, to flee from this stranger in front of them. Kieran *knew*, somehow he *knew*, and Alex hated that, hated being read as different even when they were trying to blend in with the homogenous crowd around them. Now more than ever, Alex felt they had a target nailed to their back. It was easier to run away from Kieran than to run away from themselves.

"October it is."

After they exchanged cell numbers, Alex indulged themselves with a swift kiss goodbye, made their excuses, and attempted to walk calmly into the crowd. With every step, they resisted the overwhelming urge to turn their head to catch one last glimpse of Kieran.

What Alex did catch were the cymbals crashing from a passerby's phone speaker. They tracked the tune to a couple sitting on a bench by the firehouse, listening to James Bay's "Us."

When the repeated *crash* of the cymbals accompanying Bay's words woke Alex from their stunned silence, they turned for home.

CHAPTER 3

Failure to comply with the Foundation for the Protection of Normative Gender (FPNG) will result in immediate removal from the city and mandated rehabilitation.

The FPNG was formed in accordance with our mission to protect and preserve the binaries established by normative gender.

Biological sex: Female. Failure to comply...

Presentation: Feminine (by the established FPNG standards)

Required Hormonal Makeup: Estrogen. Failure to comply...

Your Gender ID must reflect F or TF. Failure to comply...

Genders and presentations not included above are strictly prohibited.

Failure to comply...

The following Monday morning, these phrases thumped around Alex's psyche as they tried to get dressed for school. Every rebound from their brain fibers shot the words, phrases, and threats in a different direction. Racing around and around with no hope of resolution, Alex heard the words in their mind's eye as if they'd just read that FPNG poster that very morning, echoing back and forth on an unstoppable pendulum, the instance belonging to a flashback movie montage with a voiceover cautioning against rebellion.

Thus began Alex's attempt to dress for school, ticking off each normative box in their head to ensure they passed as their assigned gender: Long hair? Check. Skirt? Check. Pants? No way. It's too hot to wear pants under a skirt and the school *isn't air conditioned.* Women's tailored polo? Check. Despite there being no required school uniform, Alex's clothes felt like a uniform anyway, worn almost every day of their life, serving as a costume of assimilation.

My public presentation is itself a uniform, thought Alex in bitter realization. *What I wouldn't give to not have to make these yes or no choices just for the sake of passing under the gender radar. Things won't change anytime soon.*

Trans men: Synthetic packers required.

But what if I wanted to wear one, without having to be assigned the "trans male" gender?

What if I want short hair (found only under the Masculine Presentation category), but also wish to wear as much jewelry as I please? Being nonbinary does not necessarily mean one has to adopt an androgynous style. Alex recognized these thoughts as impossibilities. It was indeed impossible to be loudly and proudly queer without being slotted into a gender binary, a gender presentation, and forced to adhere to the rules assigned to that gender's expectations.

I still can't help but feel like I'm having a traitorous love affair with the clothes I really want to wear.

What if I want to medically transition with testosterone someday, but don't want to identify as male? What then? I'd have to prove to my parents, a therapist, countless doctors, and, worst of all, the FPNG, that I'm "binary transgender enough."

Alex recalled the torturous struggle that occurred when Ryan trying to get his testosterone injections covered by insurance when he began his medical transition. The insurance company denied him thrice on the grounds that he was "biologically female, and they only prescribe testosterone to men." It was a six-month long hassle that eventually ended with the submission of reams of paperwork from two doctors and his therapist to get the insurance to relent and cover his prescription. Just because the law requires trans men to be on T, doesn't mean all insurances, especially privately established companies, comply. The technicalities and discriminatory policies at the heart of their denial were inescapable. And, of course, who are the gatekeepers for most of these processes? Cisgender people.

The struggle is real, thought Alex. *Maybe it's for the best that I can't be on T right now, or any hormone other than estrogen. I can't imagine that fight. I saw how emotionally draining it was for Ryan. Could I endure something similar?*

These gender guidelines were the bane of Alex's existence, and they knew Juneau had felt the same way.

Alex almost envied Jo, who was assigned female at birth and seemed to have no problem with that designation. What the experience of complete acceptance of one's assigned birth gender must be like – to be assigned something at birth, the doctors, your parents, no one knowing who you are or who you want to become, and then sticking with it. Alex couldn't even imagine. More than that, what must it be like to *feel* as though you've *belonged from birth* in that designation? It was Jo's birthright not to struggle as Alex had internally.

I see you as you are. Alex remembered those words from Kieran's mouth, then remembered Kieran's mouth, his lips, their kiss.

A kiss was a kiss. It was a wonderful one, too. So much warmer and all-encompassing than the one time Ryan kissed them. Upon returning to the city, Alex had omitted Kieran from their weekend recap to Ryan, simply because they didn't want to uncork that can of worms, unleash their onslaught of bodily insecurities, and address the extreme paranoia that Kieran's parting words had instilled in them.

As you are.

The words had both chilled and frightened Alex. In their mind, they briefly replaced the word *chilled* with *thrilled*, but then backtracked. There was no greater thrill that Alex could conceive than expressing themselves and their gender(s) to the fullest extent. They still wondered what Kieran was going to say after, "I feel safe telling you this. I'm only presenting as…" Maybe they'd find out someday. Maybe they didn't want to.

What is my gender, anyway?

"Time for school, kids! Hurry up! You don't want to be late."

Jolted from their pensive trance by their dad's gentle, even voice, Alex threw on some Vans shoes. They took one last glance in the mirror, asking themselves: *Is my gender in check today? Yes. Unfortunately.*

Alex walked out into the day, steeling themselves for the mandated misgendering that school would bring.

***

After stepping off the bus at Springfield High School, Alex immediately located Ryan, and in a tired tunnel vision, met him at their lockers. As

Alex approached him, he said, "Hey there, fella," in the lowest tone he could manage.

Alex's stare could have pierced Ryan like a stinging sword. "Shhhhh! What are you doing? Are you crazy?"

"I was quiet!"

"Doesn't matter! We're in public, and even worse, we're in school." Alex glanced up at the almost-discreet black bubble cameras situated along each of the brick hallways. "You know we're being filmed."

"Are you kidding? They can't hear us. And I doubt anyone even monitors those tapes."

Alex rolled their eyes so hard they thought they'd roll out of their sockets. "It's like you *forget* what it's like. You can be so insensitive. Just because you think you have your shit together, doesn't mean we all do."

"You're doing fine. You look normal. Or, rather, you look how you're supposed to look today. What do you have to worry about?"

"Ryan, I *always* worry."

"Okay, okay. I'm sorry, Alex… Alexandra. I'm sorry."

"Thanks. And anyway, I hate the word "fella." It's not me. Just because I prefer to dress more," and their voice dropped to a whisper before they continued, "masculine, doesn't mean I like every term that comes part and parcel with that presentation."

"What about the 'Pretty Boy' tee I made you last Christmas?"

"That's different. You know I absolutely love that shirt. Just as I'm sure you don't like to be referred to in certain ways, neither do I. How would you like it if I called you bro?"

"I would hate it. That's not me."

"Exactly."

"You're right, Alexandra."

Alex flashed him a self-satisfied smirk. "I know I am."

"Shall we?"

"I suppose so. Off to another year of carefully constructed curricula."

"Hey, at least this is the last year, though? Right? We're nearly done!"

"The whole system is cyclical, Ryan. It never ends. Graduating from high school won't grant us any freedom from the FPNG and their backward standards."

Alex accepted Ryan's one-armed hug as they trod down the hallway toward their respective homerooms.

***

In Alex's second class of the day, the Intro to Sociology class offered to seniors as a primer to the required college sociology courses, the teacher uttered the most dreaded words Alex had hoped not to hear so early on in the semester.

"Okay, class. Let's jump right in, shall we? For the first couple of weeks this term, we're going to be discussing gender theory."

Alex had to physically restrain themselves from groaning out loud, especially since their seat was second in the middle row, smack-dab in the middle of the teacher's line of sight.

"Here's an easy question to get us started: who can tell me how many genders there are?"

Must we always deal in absolutes? Alex wondered.

Several hands worked their way into the air. The teacher ultimately called on Maggie, the person wearing a sweeping magenta skirt and twirling her long black hair around her middle finger. She answered, "Two! Actually, four: two main genders, male and female, and then two sub-genders, trans male and trans female."

"Very good, Maggie. Now, let's recite and record their defining characteristics."

As the teacher's voice trailed off, so did Alex. By all measure – specifically, the strict grading measures put forth by their school – Alex was a great student, achieving As and only the occasional B in years past. But at the first mention of analyzing gender guidelines and politics, Alex protested and zoned out. The diagram the teacher sketched on the whiteboard could have been taken word-for-word from any FPNG flyer. These gender guidelines permeated the threads of society so completely that no person or institution could escape them. Alex wouldn't be surprised if the school board, by order of the

FPNG, required all teachers to work their standards into every term's curricula.

Every period of Alex's day was more of the same.

In gym class, they confronted the tank top and skort uniforms that all the "girls" were required to wear. Sure, Alex loved a bright, relaxed tank, but not the kind the school issued. Alex swore that the girls' tank tops were made to be smaller, tighter, curvier, and didn't cover their chest the way the boys' tanks covered theirs.

The moment they donned the dreaded tank, they flashed back to the gender-segregated sexual education class they were required to attend upon entering high school. Skirting the class disqualified you from graduation.

"All females have a vagina, except for trans females, who…"

Says who? thought Alex.

So says the law and its bullshit foundational principles, an echo shot back in their head.

Alex couldn't be 100 percent certain, but they suspected that the few trans kids who did attend their high school, like Ryan, had been carted off for their own, separate "specialized" sex ed class. Alex and Ryan weren't friends at the time, so they didn't want to pry as to what these sessions entailed.

During the brief break between gym and weather science, Alex darted in and out of the restroom, just quickly enough to pee, wash their hands, check their sullen face for any new acne marks, and flee. Like the clothing stores, bathroom access was guarded by gender scanners, a frequent reminder of their otherness.

Alex arrived to weather science class a few minutes ahead of the bell, which sounded more like a loud, low beep over the intercom, but for some reason, students, teachers, and administrators all still referred to it as "the bell." *Words create powerful and convincing images,* Alex mused.

As the bell rang and a few stray students filed into class, Alex's ears picked up a conversation from the back corner of the room. The voices dropped to a whisper as their new teacher walked around her desk to the front of the class to begin the lesson.

"You hear about the incoming storm front headed this way?"

"No. Why? Is it bad?"

"Yeah, I wouldn't be surprised if the teach talked about it in class today."

"Should we hunker down?"

"Not sure yet. They're estimating eight to ten inches in the city proper, but that's just what I've heard."

Alex's saving grace came one period later, in English class. Running down the list of books on the syllabus that Mrs. Du Bois passed out, they zoned in on one title in particular: *Twelfth Night.* Alex knew their class wouldn't have the kind of in-depth discussion they'd idealized about fluid and free gender and gender presentation; the separation, fluidity, or combination of the two; fluid gender; nonbinary gender; free gender and presentation; breaking binaries; or deconstructing the gender hierarchy. Still, they'd rather read their favorite play yet again, which they had made a tradition of reading every summer, than read some of the other novels on the list.

I'm sure she included this as a required "classic" for the year just because it's Shakespeare. But still, I'll have to be cautious when writing assignments and essays on this one.

***

"Ready to go?" Alex approached Ryan in the cafeteria after the final bell, and from there, they walked to the long string of yellow, inner-city school buses that would deliver them home.

"Yup, just about." Ryan was clearly distracted by something on his brick of a mobile phone. "Gimme a minute."

"As long as we don't miss the bus. What is that?"

"The latest episode of *Five-Star Gaycation*."

"That show where five cis, gay guys take some poor sucker on a trip and try to make over every aspect of their life in just a week?"

"Haha, yup."

"I don't watch it."

Ryan looked up for the first time during their conversation. "Oh yeah, Alex...andra? Sounds like you do."

"I've seen snippets here and there. It's too cringey for me. Which episode is this?"

"The trans episode from their most recent season, this trans guy named Rowan."

To Alex, the branding was implicit in Ryan's explanation of the episode's differentiating factor, separating it from all the rest of the season: *The Trans™ Episode*. Alex supposed this was *Five-Star Gaycation's* attempt to appear current and inclusive.

"Yikes." As Alex scooched closer to get a better view of Ryan's screen, they caught one of the five, the sartorially inclined gay man, midway through a closet makeover for Rowan. The phrases, "born in the wrong body," and "this suit will help you look more mainstream male!" grated on Alex's ears almost as much as hearing their birth name or "she" in reference to them. "Should you be watching this here? Seems risky."

"Oh, yeah," replied Ryan. "It's been approved."

Alex couldn't take another moment of the problematic show. "This place is stifling. Let's go before we miss the bus!" Alex entwined their fingers in Ryan's and urged him to move, to which he responded, "Okay, okay. Let's go."

As they boarded their bus just in time for departure, Alex heard a low rumble of thunder from beyond their school's lush tree line. Finally, in a place of calm, distancing themselves from that wretched school day with every foot the bus drove forward, Alex sat back and smiled. *I love thunderstorms.*

CHAPTER 4

There's nothing so deliciously attractive as the sultry, inviting hug of a summer storm, Alex thought. *Thunderous in their presence and electric in their energy, they somehow invite folks to drive, walk, and run toward their dark and brooding epicenter. Prepared for it to lash out at any moment, we race into its embrace. Yet, at the very moment we run into the belly of a known beast, we ironically seek shelter the moment we sense the patter of rain. We are at once within the heart of the storm, and without.*

Storms brew even during the best of times. We take the thunderous collection of purple clouds as either a warning of imminent danger, destruction, and unease, or alternatively, we embrace the resulting fierce rain, wind, and hail as a sign of rebirth, of washing clean, weathering away the old and heralding in the new. In reality, these storms signify neither the former nor the latter; into them, we inject our own meaning.

Their nerves growing in lockstep with the storm, Alex tore their eyes away from the bedroom window. They unlocked their smartphone, and tapped the bubbly, bright green Messages icon. Alex shot off a quick text to Ryan. "We still on for tonight?"

Shutting off their phone's screen, Alex allowed themselves a brief moment to think about Kieran, about what he might be doing tonight, about where he was. Home on the coast, perhaps. Even after their short outing, Alex was sure that Kieran would have a snappy response to a text even as innocuous as this. A smile danced across Alex's lips much like the shade cast by leaves on stark, sunburnt grass. They even flirted with the idea of texting Kieran, but Ryan's reply came in and brought them back to the present.

```
R: Yup. You rethinking?

A: Not rethinking, just hesitant. I'd
rather stay home and watch the storm than
get stuck in it.
```

R: This is your chance to maybe offload some stress tho. Meet some other people like us, people you have stuff in common with.

A: And if we get caught?

R: We won't get caught - most likely

A: Most likely? Jesus, nice odds.

R: All I'm saying is, I've attended several of these youth groups with Juneau and we were fine. No danger.

A: Would be just my luck.

R: Trust me, A, we'll be okay. I think you need this. You can't hole yourself up forever. We both know that.

A: I hate that you're right. What about the storm?

R: I'm not worried. Are you?

A: About getting back I am.

What Alex didn't dare to type out was their urgent concern about malicious people tracking them down. Phone companies archived text message records that could be accessed at any time; best just to keep it vague when speaking like this, Ryan had reminded them. Still, to Alex, it looked pretty suspicious that two teenagers were out and about just as everyone and their mother were hunkering down. *Maybe there will be no one out to follow us?* Alex hoped.

After a moment of pause, in which Alex kept rewriting and backspacing their reply, they finally sent:

```
A: You're right, let's go. I'll meet you
at 6 after dinner.

R: Awesome! You know I love you. And
support you no matter what.

A: I love you, too.
```

I wonder if there's even a chance I can sneak out undetected. Alex cracked their bedroom door open ever so slightly, enough to see their dad and mum watching the news as dinner finished in the slow cooker. Distracted by the current weather report, Alex quickly lost interest in their parents. The TV's reception was already starting to crackle, presumably from the wind whipping through the trees beyond Alex's window.

"I tell ya, Dave," the meteorologist said in clipped, short sentences, "the winds are already picking up here in downtown Springfield. We're not seeing any precipitation by the harbor yet, but citizens should expect the rain to start in the next half hour or so.

"The governor is expected to issue a state of emergency, meaning any travel tonight into tomorrow night is expressly forbidden, save those folks that work in emergency services."

Fshhhhhhh. The broadcast momentarily cut to static as the storm intensified.

"The series of five blizzards we saw this past winter, followed by an unusually warm spring weakened Springfield's coastal infrastructure. Repairs to dams, sidewalks, and coastal waterways have been immediately halted as the police and fire departments put flood barriers in place, particularly on the lip of the harbor."

Fshhhhhh.

"The city will flood, the only question is just how badly. Stay tuned."

Fshhhhhh.

Alex took this latest weather interference as their cue to slink back into their room, figuring the best bet would be to sneak out after dinner.

Is it worth getting caught? Alex would surely endure severe reprimanding from their parents about sneaking out in the middle of a nor'easter. However, getting caught by something more menacing sat at the root of Alex's true fear and hesitation.

Was the opportunity to meet other nonbinary and transgender teens their age worth the risk? Would the risk pay off with more friends and emotional support and validation?

Or should they stick to the shadows for the remainder of their life?

***

The steady trickle of rain nourished the seeds of unease blooming in Alex's mind as they scaled the fire escape just outside their bedroom window two hours later. The patter against the fire escape's metal frame reminded Alex of the sound of Pop Rocks fizzing in their mouth, gentle and slight.

Waiting on the street outside their apartment building was Ryan. The moment Alex hit the pavement, the two set off for their destination.

"Did your mum drop you off?"

"Hell no," Ryan answered. "I took the train."

"Probably a safer bet. Where's this meeting again?" Alex whispered, even though there was no one in sight.

"The Sanford Sawmill."

"Yikes. That's daring, that's not too far from here."

"Yeah, well, it's abandoned," Ryan offered.

"Still."

"Alex, it's not like there are going to be FPNG officers out and about at a time like this. Plus, a large portion of the general public does their dirty work for the Foundation. And where are they now?"

"Inside?"

"Exactly."

"Mmmmm," Alex conceded.

The pair made quick work of the blocks ahead and turned back toward the river, just as the rain picked up pace. They didn't dare

48

ride the train again; there was a greater chance of getting spotted or questioned about why they were out at this hour while a nor'easter was blowing inland. They forced their way through the pinched roads, the furling waters of the approaching river threatening them from just a few feet away. Though the roads were deserted, Alex couldn't shake a mounting sense of claustrophobia; the apartment buildings and brick offices squashed Alex and Ryan as they wound their way through Springfield's meandering thoroughfares, akin to the twisting pathways that Venice, Italy boasted. But unlike Venice's cool, green, murky Mediterranean water, the echoes of the thrashing river became more apparent as they walked upstream to the sawmill.

"How did you find out about this?" Alex finally asked. "About the group?"

"I know someone. She actually runs the group."

"So, it's all by word of mouth?"

Ryan's corresponding nod sufficed as an answer as he ducked behind a particularly weatherworn and graffitied brick wall, pulling up his raincoat's hood so his face was barely visible against the dank façade and pouring rain. Alex looked up, examining the countless windows that had shattered or warped in their frames. The mill was a long-abandoned relic of Springfield's past, one which the ruthless real estate developers had yet to bulldoze.

"We're here," he mumbled.

"Already?" Just like that, the mill towered over them.

"Already. Put your hood up; we've reached our point of entry."

"Ryan, nobody's around."

"Yeah, but it's best we keep some anonymity. The place is abandoned, so there are bound to be squatters. You can never be too careful." Alex obeyed and rode Ryan's coattails as he rounded the side of the mill facing the rushing, swelling river. Ryan ducked into a doorway Alex didn't see until they were upon it, disguised by time and the deep, cloudy shadows of the evening.

Into the dank den they went, down a set of rough, iron steps, past brick room after brick room until the hallway came to a dead end.

"Here," is all Ryan said, his eyes flashing with determination as he removed his hood. Alex gingerly followed suit.

"Great place for a meeting." Alex's words were dripping with sarcasm, but they also recognized that it was perhaps the only safe meeting place in the whole metropolitan area for a gathering of illegal nonbinary folks. Not lost on them was the irony of their group – so rejected by society, so isolated because of their society's bullshit gender standards, so *abandoned* – meeting in an abandoned old sawmill.

Ryan entered the room, steadfast in his steps, with the stride of someone who's intimately familiar with a place. As he moved aside to approach someone in the far corner, Alex drank in the room in its entirety: a glorified, brick-walled storeroom, long neglected by its original owners, as evidenced by the multitude of cobwebs. Huddled on the floor in groups of two or three were the other meeting attendees.

Alex blinked hard to clear their lashes of the residual rain from their soggy journey. Most of these people, Alex noticed, were adolescents and young adults. A couple looked college age or older, but no one appeared over the age of thirty. This struck a particular chord with Alex. *Maybe older nonbinary folks who have the resources just move away from the city, as far away from this damn city as possible. As far away from detection as possible. That's a depressing thought – more isolation.*

As depressing as the scenario was, considering the circumstances, Alex marveled at this little collection of brave people. They wore a wide variety of different clothing types, and Alex presumed a variety of gender presentations. Skirts, kilts, pants, shirts, tanks, and dresses were worn by all body types. Alex merely stood there and marveled at the diversity of personal expressions: together, they made a beautiful, quilted patchwork of community.

"Alex!" At the mention of their name, Alex joined their best friend, who'd been talking to a deeper-voiced individual wearing a denim dress and combat boots, their ears crammed with as many piercings as they could fit.

Ryan wrapped his arm around Alex's shoulders as they shook hands with this person. "Alex, I'd like you to meet Shay. Shay, this is the friend I told you about."

"Talking about me, huh?" Alex said as they shot a glare Ryan's way. "All good things, I hope."

"Of course!" Shay extended her arms to give Alex a quick hug. "Ryan speaks very highly of you. Thank you for being brave and coming to our little group tonight, especially during this storm."

"You're welcome. Thank you for organizing it. You're very courageous yourself."

"What can I say? I'm a beautiful, nonbinary, transfemme Black lady who's got a lot to stick up the FPNG's ass. Since I can't *actually* do that, organizing support groups is the least I can do, considering how they've harassed me. I knew there must have been others like me."

"Yikes, I'm sorry to hear that."

Shay shrugged like the matter was nothing at all. "I'm not sorry for anything. I'm proud of who I am and refuse to apologize for that fact. I've avoided arrest so far. Want to take a seat? We're getting started in a minute."

"Sure thing," Ryan said, and he and Alex chose spots on the floor closer to the door where there was more room.

"Shay's something, huh?" Alex remarked to Ryan.

He replied, "She sure is. I'm so proud of you for coming out tonight. You know that, right?"

"I do."

Shay finished chatting with several other individuals before taking a seat at the back of the storeroom. Her even-voiced, "Thank you all for coming," shushed the group mid-chatter, and they settled in, some holding hands, some distant, some huddled close with newfound friends. She continued, "I appreciate y'all making the trek out tonight. We'll keep this month's gathering shorter than usual…"

A disappointed round of groans permeated the space.

"… because of the storm. We don't want anyone to die tonight, yeah?"

Nods all around.

Shay continued, "You all know why we're here. This is a safe space for nonbinary and gender nonconforming folks of all ages, genders, gender identities, lack of gender, what have you. We can talk about anything you want here. You are safe here; you are welcome, and you are cared for. I see we have some new faces." Shay's gaze homed in on Alex. "So, I'll introduce myself. My name is Shay, my pronouns are she/her. Why don't we go around the circle and all say our names and pronouns?"

On cue, the folks huddled in the little group took turns introducing themselves.

"Riley: she/her."

"Erin: they/them."

"Xavier: he/him."

"Dakota: ze/zir."

"Lane: he/him."

"Nova: they/them."

"Skyler: she/her."

"Winnie: e/em."

"Harper: they/them."

"Ryan: he/him."

Gulp.

"Alex: they/them."

"Thanks, all. These meetings are fairly unstructured, but as a manner of icebreaker, Ryan, would you mind starting since you've been here before?"

"Sure thing," Ryan began. "Hey, everyone. A few of you know me, but for those who do not, I'll quickly share a bit about myself and my experiences. I am a nonbinary trans man. I didn't use being nonbinary as a means to an end, as a means to becoming "fully male" or "fully a man," but I present binary now as a survival necessity. I wish my story didn't end up this way. I wish I could tell and live my story in reverse. If I did, it would sound like this:

"I consistently wore a packer to conform to the FPNG's gender standards – you all know them – otherwise I'd face penalties and persecution. One day, I encountered airport security on my way to see my grandmother in the Pacific Northwest, and I got stopped by TSA for a random strip search. The TSA official who flagged me down wanted to ensure I was packing with my prosthetic, per the law and travel guidelines, which I was. They forced my parents, also present, to allow the interrogation, threatening arrest if they, or I, refused. I was wrenched aside, taken to a private room, and strip searched by another man. They eventually released me because I was, in fact, packing.

"Upon returning home, angry and defiant from the encounter with TSA, I went out in public without packing for a few days. It was just as freeing as it was frightening. My one act of defiance, amid a lifetime of complacency.

"I desperately wish I could say that was my story, that I *was* that brave, or *am* that brave. It sounds so much more courageous in reverse. But my life is the opposite: I got caught not packing, fined, and slapped on the wrist. I arrived at my destination seven hours later and still considerably shaken up. My parents are trying, but they still call me Raya now and then.

"I'm still a man, me, Ryan, as I am and without my packer. It helps with the gender dysphoria, but I hate that I need it. I don't need a penis to define myself as a man. But, for my personal safety and protection, and for the safety of those around me, I have to."

As Ryan's last sentence rang around the room in quiet reverberations, Alex sat in deep solitude. They knew Ryan's history, of course, but to hear it now against the relief of the storm raging beyond the darkening basement windows was a different experience entirely, the timing and delivery. Ryan's eyes reflected the dirty gold glint of the dying lights overhead, boring into Alex. The light in which Alex saw Ryan, their best friend, changed too, profoundly starker and more courageous than before, though Ryan might protest at the last adjective.

"So, you're not a binary trans guy?" someone asked.

"Nope," Ryan responded. "Passing, or rather, presenting how others expect you to present for your perceived gender, isn't all there is to gender identity and living authentically."

"You do have a relative privilege, though, in your ability to pass. At least how you want to present yourself more or less aligns with the FPNG binaries," someone retorted.

"I completely agree."

Silence again, and Ryan nodded at Alex, handing off the metaphorical torch, prompting them to speak.

"I'm not exactly sure how to begin," Alex said. "I'm not sure I could follow that."

"Start anywhere you like," Shay urged. "Something that tells us a bit about you, whatever you feel comfortable sharing."

Alex took in all the faces, their ambience entrenched in swirling shades of gold and black like a faded graphic novel that a child left in the sun for weeks on end.

"Well…" A moment's hesitation, and then Alex resumed, despite their innate desire to do the contrary. "My name is Alex. I'm nonbinary. That is… that's why I'm here. I also identify as transgender, but not in any binary sense of the term. If I could choose my public presentation, it would be "masculine" as the FPNG would define it, with several adjustments. However, I don't want to be a binary guy or binary man, not to invalidate others that do. That's just not me. I would rather have testosterone in my body than estrogen, but that's an impossibility for me. Still, *I don't want to be binary*. So basically, I'm fucked. I'm not sure if this resonates with anyone here or if I'm just rambling. It's complex and I don't know how to accurately sum myself up." They shrugged, unsure of how much more information to divulge or how to continue.

Nonetheless, they forged ahead, "I haven't had clarity about who I am since I was a kid, or anything like that. My narrative is a bit of a curved arrow; no matter where I fall, I feel as if I'm constantly missing the mark. Every day feels like an assault on my body, on my identity. Every day, a new fight begins, our city warring with me over who I am and who I want to be in the future, even a year from now. I don't know how to successfully live inside any binary. In that way, I feel my days are numbered; I could be caught or expelled from Springfield at any minute. I try to keep myself 'in check' and yet I hate my life like this.

"But what terrifies me most of all is that I know someone who was taken away for who she was… is. Her capture serves as a tangible warning of the fine line I walk to exist, even attending this meeting with you all today is so dangerous. Ryan and I haven't seen her in months, and that's the only thing that could have happened to her. Even her family doesn't know where she is."

"That's terrible," Xavier said. "I know how that feels." He wore a too-big for him red and black buffalo plaid button-up with jet-black jeans and Vans. What Alex found most notable about him, other than his expressed empathy, was the thick eyeliner highlighting his radiant, hazel eyes. "I hate that I know how that feels, not belonging." Alex nodded. "How's this for laughable: The other day, my best friend, Sam, my *best friend*, actually spoke the words('I just don't understand nonbinary people. I don't have anything against them personally, other than the obvious, but they make it so hard on themselves to be who they say they are.)Why don't they just pick a gender and stick with it?' My jaw dropped. We were in public, at our favorite restaurant, so I had to recover quickly. But my *best friend* saying those words... He doesn't know about me, of course. Even if he did, I wager that he would still harbor these assumptions.

"From birth, my existence threatened the very society in which we live. I'm intersex. According to the doctors who were present at my birth, that wasn't acceptable. Mere seconds after I entered this world, when my parents were beaming with happiness and pride, they had to choose which sex, and to them, which gender I would be. The binary is upheld from birth, that much is true. To upend this system would take something monumental. So, my parents chose a gender and the doctors and nurses complied accordingly. Here I am today."

The person who introduced herself as Skyler chimed in. "We didn't choose this life. We're not making our lives harder by being who we are. The system, the city, the world, with its structures and gender rules, are the ones insisting that our existence is irrelevant. They're the ones responsible for disowning us."

"Absolutely. For how different we all are in our expressions, we do all have that in common," Shay said.

"So, I guess I'm not the only nonbinary, genderfluid person here?" Alex asked.

"Far from it," Shay said. "I am, as well. Labels can be important for our own self-definition, if they help us, but they can also be limiting."

"Tell that to the FPNG," Dakota uttered with a nervous tremor. Xavier offered zir a half-hug of comfort. Ze cleared zir throat and continued in a more even voice. "But we're not just talking about identity labels here. *Everything* for us is restricted: pronouns for those of us not comfortable with he/him or she/her, presentation, clothing…"

"Writing," Alex added. "How do you all survive, living as you are? What do you do to cope?"

Thump.

"What was that?" Alex jumped at the uncertain disturbance and looked to the others for answers.

"Sounds like something coming from the outside wall, but I can't be sure," said Ryan. "Should we…"

"*Shhhhhh.*" Shay urged. "Let's stay put. Stay quiet."

In a moment of daring, Skyler replied to Alex's previous question in a whisper, "This meeting is all I have. I know nobody else."

Just as Alex thought they heard another knock on the wall from the outside, the room's one lightbulb flickered. Its wavering gaze danced across Ryan's sallow eyes, and Alex caught his glance without thinking of it; the act was instinctual. Alex tried to turn their attention back to the group, but a sudden series of pounding sounds stopped them in their tracks, and they nearly jumped from their seat on the cement floor. Ryan seemed to be searching for an explanation for the noise just as Alex was, and Alex felt a primal sense of fear surge inside of them, followed by the urge to run. The other group members were now equally as distracted, some slowly, methodically, quietly inching toward the door.

"Who would be out right now?" Shay whispered.

Ryan said, "Well, we're out right now."

Fight or flight, isn't that what they call it? That was Alex's last thought before the dingy green door of their makeshift meeting room burst open. Alex couldn't see their faces; their blacked-out police visors both disguised them and projected an anonymity that distanced Alex from considering them individual people. The nameless threat was yelling, metal club raised, "EVERYONE STAY PUT. DOWN ON YOUR KNEES. HANDS UP!"

CHAPTER 5

Closest to the door as they were, the masked officers anchored Alex to the ground in fear. It was only as they connected their wide irises with Ryan's that an animal instinct overrode every code, every emotion, every process, and every feeling in their body and, through primal muscle memory, told them to run. In the escalating commotion of screaming and scuffling, the FPNG officers stepped toward Shay. Rather than try to save or defend her, Alex scrambled to yank Ryan's hand and flee, a last act of self-preservation.

They bolted out of the room, hung a right, and sprinted down the near pitch-black hallway toward the wrought iron staircase, ready to ascend from their basement hideaway to the outside world and into the nor'easter awaiting them. They could disappear into the chaos of the storm if they could only get that far.

Behind them, Alex heard one of the FPNG officers growl, "Hey! We've got two escaping! I'm going to pursue!"

"No! You stay here. The rest are trapped, let's just round up those we have." Alex barely caught the commanding officer's reply as the sentence echoed down the damp, empty hallway.

They are trapped, Alex realized, the only thought currently coursing through their mind other than the urge to flee. *It's the room at the end of the hallway. They're trapped in there.*

Ryan slowed his pace and barked out a hoarse plea. "We need to go back! Shay! The others!"

"No time," was all Alex could manage.

They flew up the stairs, two at a time, and threw their bodies at the door. Gone were the pitter patter of lazy rain drops. Alex and Ryan tumbled out into an icy bath of torrential, driving rain with no end in sight. The storm was as urgent as their fear, heavy sheets of rainfall beating their heads, with flash after flash of lightning crackling above.

Alex's flight instinct coursed through them like new blood, a transfusion of unbridled adrenaline that empowered them to keep Ryan clutched in one of their hands as they dragged him along, shocked and legs still stumbling to match their pace. Ryan's sloshing footsteps sputtered to a halt, thrusting Alex forward alone, just as they caught sight of a double-folded piece of paper ripping its way through the raging wind. Ryan's searching eyes desperately traced the paper's path.

Alex yelled, "What?! What are you stopping for? We need to haul ass!"

Ignoring them, Ryan vaulted over a nearby bus bench and lunged for the damp, limp paper, his treasure. He took a deep, steadying breath, and then returned his attention to Alex and joined them in sprinting away from the sawmill.

"What do you think you're doing?" Alex shouted.

"It's Juneau's letter."

"What letter?"

"She wrote me before she left."

Aghast, Alex huffed, "What? Do you carry it around with you all the time? Did she say where she…"

"No specifics, just that she loves me and promised she'd stay safe."

The splashing rain disguised both pairs of their heavy footfalls. That very disguise could equally camouflage anyone – *The police? The FPNG? Did it matter the difference?* – following *them*. Ryan's sprint finally caught up with Alex's, but he didn't let go of their hand. The pair left city block after city block in their dust before they realized their inadvertent destination: the northernmost end of Springfield Harbor, which was due to flood any moment. The rainwater sloshed higher and higher up their ankles, slowing them down.

"Is anyone chasing us?" Alex yelled over the roar of the rain and approaching waves, thick with seafoam and capped with the roiling promise to break over the harbor's reinforced barriers.

"I don't know! But the ocean's about to swallow us whole if we get any closer! We don't want to get caught in the riptide!"

"What do you suggest? Go back?"

"Hunker down somewhere here!"

Alex whipped their head around and around, fueled by the pounding wind, searching for solace from the storm, the rising tides at their feet, and now, apparently, the FPNG. Were they a fugitive? Should Alex and Ryan flee the city altogether? Should they head back to Alex's apartment for shelter, then leave at night? Alex didn't know the status of their long-term safety, so instead chose to focus on the immediate danger at hand.

"There!" Alex screamed over the howling in their ears. They could barely hear themselves, and they had no idea if Ryan could make out their words. "The coffee shop!" Taking a moment to jab their finger at Rainbow Club Coffee, a small, local joint set just two blocks from the harbor's edge, Alex dragged Ryan along and they climbed cautiously through the shattered frame of what used to be the shop's front window, damaged from the wicked storm.

The pair plopped down on the far side of the shop against the coffee bar, pooped, bedraggled, and completely soaked to the bone.

"Ironic, isn't it?" Ryan gasped in short, shallow breaths.

"Huh? What?" Alex struggled to catch their breath and slow their pounding heart.

Ryan managed a cynical half-smile. "Two queer fugitives taking refuge in a downtown coffee shop owned by a lesbian couple."

"Their gender isn't illegal, they're fine."

"You got me there."

"Man, Kieran would be surprised that I got myself into a situation like this. I think he thinks I'm not adventurous or something."

"Who?"

"Oh, that's right." *I never told Ryan about him.* "Kieran's just this guy I met when I was in York."

"Just some guy, huh? Why didn't you tell me about him?"

Why didn't *I tell Ryan about him? What did I think I was keeping from him?* "I dunno, must have slipped my mind. We hung out for a little, that's all."

Ryan's winning, warm smile pierced Alex. They wouldn't be able to shrug off their best friend for much longer. "And...?"

"And we kissed. But that's it."

"So, the truth comes out! When do I get to meet him?" Alex couldn't help but laugh at the absurdity of the entire situation. There they were, sheltering from the storm of their lives, on the run from the FPNG, probably fugitives or being hunted, and Ryan thought it most urgent to talk about a random guy with whom Alex spent one evening.

"You're unbelievable, you know that? I don't know when. He wants to visit me, but I don't know if I should let him."

"Why?"

"Umm, because of this whole situation. And…" Alex trailed off, looking around the deserted café as a matter of reflex, to see if anyone was listening.

"And?"

"And before we parted, one of the last things Kieran said to me was, 'I feel like I see you the way you want to be seen, not as everyone else sees you.' That's some scary shit, Ryan. What if he *knows*?"

"That's impossible, Alex. How could he? Not unless you said something…"

"Are you nuts? I would never. He's very attractive, but confessing something like that to a stranger, someone you just met, is risky and I don't like taking my chances."

"You certainly took one tonight, so you can't tell me that you're totally risk-averse, Alex."

Alex rolled their eyes, recalling that they'd felt the same hesitation earlier this evening before sneaking out of their bedroom window. "Well, I took the risk tonight and look where it landed us. It figures, the moment I decide to share a part of myself and my struggle with someone other than you, shit goes down. Can it really be a coincidence?"

"At least we're together."

"We are."

***

"Where the hell were you two?" Ryan's mom thundered the moment they opened the door to Alex's apartment.

Ryan and Alex sulked, soaking from both rain and sweat, and sodden in both body and spirit. They stood dripping on the family doormat, face to face with both sets of their parents. Alex and Ryan caught them mid-pacing, mid-calling, mid-panic as they searched frantically for their missing children.

"I'd like to know the same thing," Alex's dad chimed in, arms crossed, which was quite uncharacteristic. *He must be pissed.*

Ryan sighed and stepped forward. "We got caught out in the storm."

"That's obvious. Come in." Ryan's mum urged him forward and sat him down on the couch, leaving Alex to shiver in the doorway. "Where were you?" she asked again, eyes darting between Alex and her son. Alex's lips were frozen from terror as much as from the cold, crystallizing sleet.

"Here, come in, come in," Alex's dad ushered them inside the apartment, then firmly shut and deadbolted the door. "Your mother and I were scared shitless."

"We were out with some friends," Ryan offered weakly.

I can lie better than that, Alex thought bitterly. *If only I could bring myself to.*

Ryan's mum suddenly rounded on Alex, mere inches from their face, and yelled, "Where did you take my son?"

"Mom, calm down! Alex didn't take me anywhere! It was my suggestion!"

"Then. Where. Were. You?"

I can't let Ryan take complete fault for tonight.

A brief pause fell over the group, and Alex thought they could hear the tears pouring off their chin and collecting in puddles on the floor where they stood. "We went to a secret meeting for nonbinary folks."

Plop.

Alex's mum whispered, "That can't be true."

"It is," they replied, and hung their head in sorrow, in mourning. *The one good thing I had. Briefly, for a moment.*

Now what happens?

PART 2

REFLECTIONS IN THE DOVE PRISM

CHAPTER 6

Springfield's vibrant patchwork of foliage brimmed against a deep sky-blue horizon and complemented the steady afternoon breeze. From microcosm to macrocosm, each singular fallen autumn leaf, like the wider skyscape itself, contained its own unique brushstrokes of bronze, sunny yellow, burnt orange, scarlet, and any chlorophyll that remained, the dying embers. The foliage's pigmentation, leaf by leaf, varied in a beautiful kaleidoscope of fall hues.

October was always so warm, inviting, and tangible to Alex. There was something about that tenth month, the late fall ambience, the cocktail of pumpkins, the crunchy autumnal leaves, scarves and sweaters, warm lattes and warmer hugs, and the spookiness of the season – Alex loved it all. One of the sounds they cherished most, especially in their late teen years, was the sound of rustling leaves on dying trees, crisp and hollow and exclusive to the fall, where the rustle sounded akin to a gentle sheet of falling rain, so delicate it appeared as a stream of mist. Somehow, the husky tunes were as haunting as they were sublime.

Xavier. Riley. Dakota. Erin. Winnie. Harper. Skyler. Lane. Nova. Shay.

Wonderful human beings. A community in their own right. Alex mourned the loss of each of them.

They turned each individual's name over and over in their mind as they witnessed the leaves' afternoon shadows dance across their bed, craving Ryan's presence. Alex felt like they were in the theater, witnessing the finale of an exotic dance piece, the leaves shuddering as the crisp autumn wind whipped its way through their hair.

It's been a month already.

"Did someone say they were missing me?" Alex's body jolted at the surprise voice, and they found Ryan slinking his way through their open window from the fire escape.

"Jesus, Ryan, you scared the crap out of me!"

"You said you wanted to see me, so here I am."

"I'm surprised you'd dare to sneak out. Especially with what happened."

Ryan offered Alex a cool smile before swiftly kissing them on the cheek and playfully bopping them on the nose. "It wasn't easy, but I wanted to see you, too. It was my fault we got caught anyway."

"I went, though," Alex said, sullen and dejected as they recalled the terror-laced memories. They sat up and turned to face Ryan as he reclined in Alex's bed, his hands laced behind his head. "My one chance of meeting other friends, people like us..."

Shifting the subject of the conversation, Alex asked, "Why are you so chipper?"

"Why aren't you? Our month of grounding is almost over!"

"Yeah, true. I'd almost rather stay inside. No one can see me here. I'm just scared, Ryan. I'm scared everywhere I go that some FPNG official, or even some random person, is going to recognize me and..."

"Did they get your name? Fingerprint you?"

"Well, no."

"Then they can't prove anything. You know that."

"I'm still on high alert, though," Alex admitted.

"Makes sense."

Alex knew they would regret pushing the issue and wished they could shrug it off, but they couldn't help but ask, "What about Shay? Aren't you worried?"

Ryan closed his eyes and sighed heavily. "Alex, *of course* I am. Honestly, the only reason I'm not in a depressive hole right now – first Juneau and now Shay – is that I try not to think about it."

"I wish I could do that. I'd give anything to block out the memories of that night."

Ryan's voice dropped an octave as he assumed a dourer tone. "It haunts me, it does. But there's nothing I can do."

"I refuse to believe that. There *must* be something we can do to help them."

"On another note, why are you wearing your street clothes? You know, the FPNG's definition of feminine clothes you loathe and only wear in public? Are your parents making you? I can talk to them."

Ryan gave Alex a quick once-over, taking in their gray V-neck tee, black cardigan, maroon corduroy slacks, and jet-black skirt. "I'm digging the corduroy, though."

"No, no. Listen to me."

"I'm listening."

"Are you? Then hear what I am saying. My parents aren't making me do anything. I'm wearing these clothes because I don't feel safe anymore, even in my own house, my own room. These places used to be my safe havens – hell, even your apartment felt safe. But not anymore. I'm not safe anywhere."

From Alex's stereo alarm clock, Bastille sang about seeing a change racing through their minds with the singer unable to recognize the person's face they desperately tried to remember, seasonal changes supplanting their recollections.

"Alex, you're safe with me."

"Don't use that name."

"I will! Alex *is* your name."

"Ryan."

"Do you feel safe with me?" he persisted.

Alex rolled their eyes and said, "Of course I do. I never said that I didn't, with you specifically. I just worry that at any moment, the police could burst in thanks to the betrayal of a teacher or some kid in my class or the FPNG itself and accuse me of being who I am."

Ryan lashed back. "And what do your parents say? Huh? Do they think the same as you?"

Another vicious eye roll, and Alex pulled further away from Ryan and crossed their arms. "They say that as long as we weren't caught and they didn't confiscate our IDs, we are fine. But they forbade me from ever going to those meetings again. They don't need to convince me anyhow; I'm done with them. I never should have gone."

"It's okay to wear what you want in secret!"

"No, Ryan, it's not. I know I'm nonbinary genderfluid. You know. My parents know. If someone else doesn't betray me, what if I betray myself?"

Ryan gripped their shoulders a bit harder than intended and forced Alex to look directly into his eyes. "You won't betray yourself, and neither will I. Okay?" The intensity of his stare drew small tears from Alex's eyes, and they weakened.

"Okay," they relented, "fine."

"You're safe here," Ryan reiterated. "But if you want to check for bugs and mini recording devices, I'm your guy. Okay?"

"Okay."

"I'm sure Jo would back me up on this. You need some gender euphoria in this binarized, bullshit world we live in. I'll leave if you want to get changed."

Dragging themselves out of their depressive stupor, Alex relinquished some of their stubbornness. "No need, you've seen me undress before."

"Your choice. Now, tell me more about this Kieran guy." The sound of his name plucked an effortless smile from the corners of Alex's frown, though the temptation of forgetting about Kieran or cutting him out entirely pricked at their mind.

***

"I can't believe you're finally here. The summer feels like ages ago, not just two months." Alex sat lust-struck across the table from Kieran, who looked more handsome than ever in dark blue suede dress shoes, black skinny jeans, a black V-neck, and a sky-blue buffalo plaid scarf. They couldn't help but wonder how Kieran's relative performative masculinity afforded him more ease in navigating his world than Alex, both in identity and presentation. Comparatively, Alex felt frumpy, dowdy even, but Kieran didn't seem to bat an eyelash. *I wish I looked more like you. At first, I wondered if I was attracted to you or if I simply wanted to* be *you. But now, I know it's both.* Slender orange shafts of autumn sunlight cut across their table, highlighting their own copper and obsidian Halloween plaid shirt.

"Finally? So, you missed me, huh?" Two pumpkin spice cappuccinos sat between the pair.

"Of course I did, you goof. How've you been?"

"Fine, same as always. I'm sure the city's more exciting than where I'm from."

"No way. I'd rather sequester myself by the ocean."

Kieran snorted into their cappuccino, nearly spewing the foamy milk and pumpkin seasoning all over his face. "The ocean? You know that tons of tourists and pseudo-locals flock to the beaches in the summers, yourself included. Southern Maine's gotten quite claustrophobic in the last five years or so. There is no sequestering to be had."

Alex rolled their eyes over and over in response. "Yeah, yeah, yeah. But there are a hell of a lot fewer people there than in Springfield."

"And I happened to meet the most charming one." Kieran winked dramatically. "Listen." He leaned in so his nose was mere inches from Alex's. They wondered with glee if he was about to kiss them again. "I have something to tell you. But not here. Can we go back to your place?"

Alex obliged and led Kieran by the hand to their apartment. They swiftly introduced him to their parents and then quickly locked them into their back bedroom. When they were alone, Kieran resumed his confession.

He glanced out Alex's window reflexively. "You won't catch me saying something like this in public, but I'm nonbinary – agenderflux and transfemme, to be specific."

"I knew it!" Alex practically shouted, then clapped a hand over their mouth. "I knew it," they repeated, but quieter this time. "Is that what you were trying to tell me that night on the Ferris wheel?"

"Nonbinary, yes," Kieran finished with a genuine, wide smile. He barely breathed the word.

Alex placed a careful hand on Kieran's knee. "I wish I could congratulate you and say, 'That's amazing!' but under the current circumstances…"

"I know."

"But since we're not out in public…"

"You want to know? I'll tell you, Alexandra."

"Please, Alex."

"That's more like it. You don't seem much like an Alexandra anyway. In the very small, safeguarded circles in which I've divulged my identity to others, just a couple of friends and some allies, I've said that I'd love nothing more than to tell the world I'm proud of being a nonbinary, transfemme person. I present very femme in secret, mostly only with those friends."

Alex's mind instinctively substituted Kieran's skinny jeans for a skirt, and they blushed at how attractive Kieran looked in any clothing.

"That's just how I prefer to dress. However, I don't see me being nonbinary as something necessarily tied to how I dress. I'm happier dressing certain ways than others, but I'm nonbinary in my own right, regardless of presentation."

"What do you mean?"

"Nonbinary doesn't mean that a person necessarily adheres to a certain kind of gender presentation or other. I don't need to dress in any one way to signify that I am nonbinary. Like many of us, my clothing does not constitute my gender identity. I, Kieran, am nonbinary as I am."

What a wonderful way of thinking about oneself.

"That's amazing. I love that. So, what are your pronouns?"

Kieran laughed at the question and said, "Well, seeing as how strangers read me as a guy, male, man, whatever, I have to endure people calling me 'he' all the time. I'm pretty okay with all pronouns, but I prefer they/them."

"Me too!" Forgetting themselves, the exclamation fell out of Alex's mouth before they could prevent it.

Kieran laughed again. "You're adorable. I knew it would be safe to tell you."

"And the great conspiracy spreads. Outside of my family and my best friend Ryan, no one close to me knows my pronouns, or that," they dipped their voice to a whisper, "I'm nonbinary, genderfluid, I joke, but I know too well the illegality of even saying these incriminating things."

"You always like to bring things back to reality, don't you, Alex?"

"For good reason." As Alex's meek voice trailed off, so did their eyes, and they withdrew themselves from Kieran.

"I'd hate to have to call you 'she' in public again, using those wrong pronouns to reference you."

Alex sighed deeply. "Yeah, well you have to. I don't know what it's like out of state, but we're watched closely here in Springfield. Living in the city means navigating a minefield, always being one wrong word away from discovery. You have to refer to me as she/her."

Kieran reached back for them, asking, "Did something happen?"

"Yeah. Well, technically, something *almost* happened. I almost got caught attending a meeting for nonbinary folks at the city's abandoned sawmill."

"Jesus Christmas, that was daring of you. Seems out of character, based on the little I know about you so far."

"I waffled back and forth on whether to go, but ultimately decided that I wanted more camaraderie and to meet more friends instead of holing myself up in mine and Ryan's bedrooms for the remainder of senior year."

"So, what happened?"

"It was raided, no idea how, but word spread to someone. The FPNG showed up and kicked down the door in the middle of that nor'easter. Ryan and I got away, but I think the rest of the group was captured. Raw, in-my-bones terror. That night shook me. Ever since then, I just have this gut feeling that I'm being watched."

"We're all being watched, always," Kieran pointed out. "But that's a horrendous thing to endure. I'm so sorry, Alex."

"Yeah, well, I think they're watching me a bit extra now. I trust my gut on this. So, I present as the model female schoolgirl, perfectly adherent to the law in every way."

"Hmmm, I don't know…" The skepticism in Kieran's long pause was clear. "A gut feeling is just that: a feeling. You don't have any proof."

"I don't need proof to be suspicious or to presume that I'm in danger. Just promise you'll use the correct pronouns in public, okay?"

Kieran joked, "You mean they/them, right?" Despite the playful tone in their voice, Alex felt like slapping them for chiding their very real warning.

71

"No. She/her. I'm serious." Alex felt shitty for calling Kieran out, but they were acting like a naïve child.

"I know, I know. I'm sorry. Let me make it up to you, Alex. I know what will cheer you up."

"What could that be? Other than your stunning presence, of course." Kieran couldn't mistake the cutting sarcasm in Alex's tone, veiling their affection for them with feigned annoyance.

"Let's have a night in."

"Like Netflix and chill? Pizza and YouTube?"

"A *date* night in. I'm asking you out, Alex."

"Oh." Flabbergasted, Alex's mouth hung open a little, and they couldn't think of how to reply other than, "Of course! I would love that. I mean, I would like that very much."

"How are you so freaking adorable?"

"I don't know, how are you?" A brief chuckle and then Alex said, "But where?"

"My uncle's place, of course."

"Which is… where?"

"In Springfield, actually, I'll give you the address if you want to jot it down."

Alex's stomach started to writhe, equally anticipatory and anxious. "But he doesn't know… he can't know…"

Kieran waved off their concerns, not bothered by them in the slightest. "He's out of town for the night. This way, you can dress exactly how you want. As can I. How's tonight?"

"It's a date."

CHAPTER 7

"Alex, what are you doing here?"

"School, Ryan, same as any other Monday."

"I mean, what are you doing here like *that*? You're, umm… not dressed."

"Of course I'm dressed. I have clothes on, don't I?" their annoyance transparent in their barking tone.

Ryan's eyes darted back and forth between Alex and the other students flocking up and down the main corridor before the first bell. The eyes of their classmates fell increasingly on the pair, to Alex's great consternation.

"I mean, you're not *dressed*," he emphasized in hushed tones, then hissed, "Get out of here, now! Before the principal…"

"Miss Cesario!" Principal Hatchett's booming voice cut across the morning chatter to Alex's ears, and only then did they realize they were dressed in traditionally male clothes.

***

Two weeks before…

After Kieran left Alex's house, Alex paced nervously. Were they really going to spend an evening with Kieran, and be *exactly* who they are? Was it safe? Was it wise? Would they regret the venture much like the sawmill mishap? The excitement finally got the better of them, and with conviction and a few butterflies, they opened the closet to choose what to wear that night.

After spending the afternoon with their best friend, gushing over all the details, Alex ditched Ryan's house early. He sarcastically rolled his eyes, but was genuinely happy for Alex that they were finally leaving their self-imposed prison with a bag of their best clothes. Unaccustomed to dedicated date nights, their only dressing criteria were selecting the clothes in which they felt most like themselves.

On the journey to Kieran's uncle's apartment, downtown near the waterfront in a prestigious neighborhood known as Chestnut Hill, they nervously gripped their phone and listened to the GPS app that was cheerily spitting out directions. Though they had a slight inkling of the apartment's direction, Alex still kept the GPS on, but at a low volume; they hated being suspected of not knowing every sector of their own city.

Alex's Vans shoes pounded the pavement, both anxious and eager to transform their appearance and finally validate their true genderfluid, nonbinary trans self. Their anxiety was laced with glee as they anticipated stripping from dysphoric to euphoric clothing, waiting for the moment when it was safe to step into Kieran's presence as themselves. Alex lived two lives: one public and one private. As they crossed the narrow, cobblestone street to Kieran's uncle's apartment, a picturesque, New England structure with a red-brick Georgian façade, Alex marveled at the poetry of their life's duality.

Before tonight, I couldn't conceive of these two lives intersecting, the private somehow interrupting the public. But here we are.

***

What was Saturday's gender euphoria – proudly wearing a midnight-blue, polka-dotted button-up and men's skinny jeans, long hair tucked up into a gray beanie, sitting across from Kieran at a candlelit table for two on their uncle's street-facing balcony – evolved into Sunday's usual skirt and V-neck shirt with a slight ruffle weighing down the sleeves. All that remained of Saturday's look were the Vans shoes.

Saturday's euphoria was Sunday's dysphoria. Alex attempted to cling to the former feeling, to the image of Kieran with their sexy scruff and a skirt that hugged their hips and legs in all the right ways, their large, golden-backed pearl earrings projecting the essence of old Hollywood glamor. But it was no use. Dysphoria reigned.

Saturday's happiness transformed into the Sunday Scaries. Sure, Alex still sat across from Kieran at the dinner table on Sunday, their last meal of the weekend, but it was in public at Alex's favorite pizzeria, La Bocca Forte. The ecstasy of Kieran and Alex exchanging their preferred pronouns in private suddenly turned lethal as Kieran mistakenly spoke those same they/them pronouns aloud once more, but this time, to the waiter taking their dessert order.

Still riding high from the fabulous queerness that was Saturday night, Kieran only realized that they'd said anything amiss after, "They'll have the tiramisu," came out of their mouth, accompanied by gesturing both hands at Alex.

"Excuse me, sir?" The waiter offered a look of kind dismay.

"Huh? I, uh…" Kieran stammered, for some reason looking to Alex for the right response.

Maybe we're fine, Alex thought. *Maybe the waiter really didn't catch what Kieran said. Maybe he thought it was an honest stumble and will let the moment pass.*

But the waiter continued, "What did you just call her?" *Or maybe not. Unmistakable. He caught it. He caught me.*

"Yeah, Kieran. What did you just call me?" Alex recovered themselves in time to respond with a chuckle, trying to play it off. "I swear, your head is in the clouds today."

"Sorry, I was thinking about two things at once. She will have the tiramisu, and I'd like the lemon ricotta cake."

Yesterday. Yesterday. Yesterday.

Yesterday, Kieran's uncle walked in earlier than expected as Kieran and Alex were finishing their dinner, before Alex had changed back into their street clothes. For once, they hadn't worried about the exposure because Kieran had endlessly assured Alex their uncle knew Kieran was nonbinary, too.

But now they were worried.

Yesterday.

Alex's already pale complexion was now ghostly white, reflecting the bitter chill that sat on their chest. Their energy and their affection for Kieran drained from them in equal measures.

Sunday's breach of protocol squashed Saturday's sense of security with an anvil weighted with reality. *Was Kieran the threat I never saw coming? It was an accident, but I can't afford a single one.*

Forcibly drawing their mind back to the table, Alex saw the waiter jot down their respective dessert orders in swift strokes and depart. But by his last lingering glance, they swore he could have been

75

writing down their names. He could have noted them from servicing their table and overhearing their conversations.

Both the waiter and Kieran left their eyes lingering on Alex.

"Alexandra, I…"

"Please shut up." *Betrayal.* They continued under their breath. "Don't say another word. Until he comes back. Then, act normal."

Alex desperately longed for a pause on dinner, a pause on life, time to MacGyver their way out of this situation. A pit of dread churned in their stomach when they remembered that their ID number and name were cataloged in La Bocca Forte's customer relationship management (CRM) system from when they keyed into the women's restroom.

The waiter returned a few short moments later, dessert in hand, and asked to see both Alex and Kieran's IDs.

"Alexandra V. Cesario?" he asked, pointing his finger at Alex as they forked over their ID.

"Yes, that's me."

"Female? Aged eighteen?"

"Yes, sir. It says so right there."

The waiter squinted at Kieran's own ID picture, and began, "So, what…" he squinted once again. "Kieran Orsino. What were you two talking about before I came over to grab your dessert order?"

"Sir?" Kieran finally joined the conversation. "I don't understand what you're asking."

"Mr. Orsino, I heard you refer to this young lady," jabbing an accusatory finger at Alex, "as they. Is that true? Why did you say that? What were you two talking about?"

This can't be happening. Raw denial was the only tool within Alex's reach that kept them anchored in the present, that kept them from going totally ballistic.

Kieran's back was against the wall. "I'm not sure. We were talking about Alexandra's parents and how much they love this restaurant. I don't remember saying it," they lied. If this were a sparring match, Kieran would have been pinned to the ground two seconds ago. Alex felt Kieran backpedal as they ran their mouth. "Alex…andra's pronouns are she/her."

Kieran, what is wrong with you? Dig my grave too, why don't you.

"Precisely." The waiter smirked unconvincingly. "Here you are, enjoy your dessert." He left their plates and returned their IDs.

***

"Ryan, I swear, in the moments between the waiter leaving and returning with dessert, I was numb. Like my whole body was shot with Novocain."

"Geez."

"So numb. I wasn't sure the waiter heard what Kieran said at first, but then he came back. He can't know anything, all he has is conjecture, right?" Alex doubted themselves even as they uttered the words.

"Alex, this whole damn system operates, no, *is predicated on* suspicion and conjecture."

"What the hell am I supposed to do now? I'm terrified. I left Kieran outside the restaurant and barely mumbled a goodbye to them."

"I'm coming over. If something happens, and I'm not saying anything is going to happen, I want to be there. Maybe you'll get lucky and you won't get served."

"Maybe."

Click.

Alex hung up and immediately regretted calling Ryan in a panic. What if someone in the park had overheard their conversation? They huddled in a ball on the stone bench at the far end of Springfield's Public Gardens, the brilliance of the flowers' spring glory long faded with the inception of fall, and not even the sight of the public works folks setting up for the Harvest Festival cheered Alex. In that moment, with biting horror and fright, they realized that their phone could have been tapped. The FPNG had free rein to monitor all calls. Would they be on Alex's case this fast? Were the cogs of the machine that well-greased? Or did Alex overestimate them? Was this all just skeptical paranoia, festering from the night at the sawmill?

No such luck in this life. I'm spiraling.

Forced out of the gardens by the setting sun, Alex swung their apartment door open a half hour later, expecting a bear hug from Ryan. Instead, Alex was ungraciously greeted by the stern face of an officer, who was adorned in a plain black uniform and hat brandishing the four letters Alex dreaded most. They felt bolted onto the welcome mat.

Staring at the officer, Alex noticed her bun was wound so tight that it must have been cutting off circulation to her brain. *Are FPNG officers trained to dull their sympathy for those they target? Who would choose to take up such a post? Do they have a choice? Are they just cogs in the machine themselves?* To Alex, everyone was a willing participant in the system. Hell, they were just as much a willing participant in perpetuating the status quo as anyone else. Alex played their public role, until now. The FPNG didn't lack for volunteers; with their fingertips outstretched across the entirety of their society's infrastructure, so embedded in every person and every institution, nails dug in, Alex speculated that the organization didn't require as many FPNG officers as they'd originally assumed. Every civilian was an unwitting volunteer.

"This warning is for you," she said, then handed Alex a manila business envelope addressed to them, turned on her heel, and marched out before they could offer a retort.

Not being willing to wait for Ryan, Alex slammed the door, ripped open the envelope, swiftly discarded the FPNG gender standards flyer included, and prayed to the gods that their parents were still gone on their upstate college reunion trip. Alex scanned the letter.

Dear Ms. Alexandra V. Cesario,

It has come to the attention of the Foundation for the Protection of Normative Gender (FPNG) that at 5:37 this evening, an incident involving your person was reported at La Bocca Forte of Springfield, Massachusetts. The incident was reported as a Class C breach of FPNG guidelines, as enforced by the aforementioned city.

*The letter is your formal reminder that further breaches
of FPNG guidelines will result in significant financial
penalties, and should the threat prove persistent, your
arrest.*

Alex gulped at the "*your arrest*" part. The letter continued:

*For the full list of our guidelines, to which you commit to
comply and to which you are bound as a lawful citizen,
please visit our website or visit one of our Springfield
branch offices. If you need assistance complying with
these mandatory guidelines, we would be happy to
assign you a state-licensed therapist.*

*Should you fail to fully comply with the law as
prescribed by the FPNG, further action will be taken
in due course.*

> *Wishing you well,*
>
> *Violet Vigil*
> *Associate Director*
> *FPNG's Springfield Branch*

***

"I'm running out of lives, Ryan!" Alex barraged him with exclamations as soon as he stepped through the door, not long after Alex had finished reading their letter.

"Hold on, hold on. Let me come in first. It's already getting dark out and my bones are freezing."

"Yes, yes, that happens every fall. Now look!" Alex shoved the official notice, FPNG seal and all, under Ryan's nose, nearly giving him a paper cut.

Alex blew out the longest and most dramatic guffaw of their life. "I'm screwed. I bit the big one, and it wasn't even my fault! But because of others' mistakes! There have been too many slipups where I'm concerned."

Ryan offered what was supposed to pass for a supportive shrug. "Shit. We don't know just how bad it is yet."

"Oh, PUH-lease. Bad enough for them to hand-deliver me *that*." Alex flicked the letter, now in Ryan's hands. "I need to take stock of the situation and fast. Kieran screwed me. So much for claiming to like me. We barely slipped out of their clutches at the sawmill, but this is unforgivable."

"Woah, woah. I'm not telling you to calm down, just try to take a breath. I feel like you're going to come out swinging any minute."

"Me, too, Ryan. I'm about to have a full-on panic attack."

"Shit. We need to keep you safe, Alex. I'll keep you safe."

"So much for keeping me safe. So, do you finally admit that attending that meeting was a bad idea? Even if your friend was the one who ran it?" Alex regretted directing their blame at Ryan; he didn't report them to the police, after all. But without a clear suspect, surely someone had to accept fault for this.

"Yes, I regret it now, especially considering the outcome and the state it left you in. Do you regret seeing Kieran?"

He had to ask. "Yes. Maybe. I don't know! I give up." Alex flung themselves on the living room couch like a Victorian dandy throwing themselves on a divan, only instead of embracing the sweet taste of champagne that would be waiting on a glass side table, all Alex could taste was the bitter, metallic flavor of impending disaster and forthcoming arrest.

"No," Ryan insisted. "Don't give up. Not yet. I can't lose you, too."

"Ryan, what the hell am I supposed to do? Hide for the rest of my life? What happens when all of these missteps converge?"

With infinite regret for what he must say, Ryan answered, "You need to stay the course. Convince them you're Alex*andra*. Female and all that, however horrendous that may be. Then maybe those missteps won't converge."

Alex's crestfallen, pleading look spoke for them. "For how long?" they asked quietly.

"Until we can get out of here, after Springfield High. You'll still have to make public appearances now and again, but we'll find some remote place. Just you and me."

"Just you and me."

"Alex?"

"Yeah?"

"Just promise me you'll be safe. Stay low. You know I won't slip up. I love you too much. I hate that we have to play this charade, but…"

"But what?"

"But for you, I'd do anything. Are you going to tell your parents about this?"

"No. It's better they don't know for now. Trust me."

***

The weeks soared by as the now-deceased autumn leaves fled their branches, and Alex couldn't shake the feeling that they were still being watched. They didn't know for certain, but it was better to be safe than sorry that they didn't heed their hand-delivered prison sentence warning. The fun spookiness of Halloween was replaced with the constant dread one feels when anticipating a jump scare, an unseasonable chill up Alex's spine and considerable sweat on their back.

Ever the acutely observant younger sister, Jo cornered Alex daily with concern and questions. Even under the watchful eyes of their close friends and family, Alex withdrew further and further from the bosom of their protection.

"Would running away help?" Alex murmured in low tones to Ryan on the phone. "What about self-sabotage? Let my family off the hook and just turn myself in to save you, them, and all of us the frustration in the end?"

"Alex, what the hell?" Ryan's booming reply passed clear through the door.

"What was that?" Jo shouted.

"Nothing! Go back to watching *House Hunters!*" Alex responded. Turning their back to the door as if doing so to Ryan, they admonished him. "Are you kidding me? Keep it down!"

"If you're so worried about being overheard, why are you talking about this over the phone?"

"Don't turn this back on me."

Ryan released a long, breathy sigh from the other end. "Look, Alex. Do you remember when I told you that I don't want to lose you? Shit, that I can't lose you?"

"Yes."

"I meant it. Don't self-sabotage. It would solve absolutely nothing, and more importantly, it would risk your safety. They'd arrest you, reform you, ship you back here, and 'reorient' you. You'd be back to square one. How would that feel?"

"Ryan, that's what they say, but we haven't seen Juneau since… we don't know when, right?"

"Don't."

"It's true! Maybe she resisted a bit too much."

Another long sigh crackled through Alex's phone speakers. Outside, they heard the strong thrum of a motorcycle zoom down their street, its echo reverberating through the bars of Alex's fire escape like a gust through wind chimes.

If only I could escape, too. Without a scratch. Without notice.

"Either way, that's all the more reason you need to stay put and not make any rash decisions. Let's not focus on her right now, Alex. Let's focus on you, and keeping you sane and safe. Okay?"

"Okay."

"So, what can you do tonight to help you recover from the bullshit of the month? You haven't written in a long time. Maybe that? Or read a non-school book?"

Alex chuckled to themselves. Leave it to Ryan to ignore the bad and focus on inane distractions. "Yeah," Alex eventually admitted. "I could write."

"You said it once, Alex, writing is your only escape for now. Try to live vicariously through your writing and exercise some sense of creativity. It might refresh you."

"I'll try, but I definitely can't leave my journal out where people could find it."

"Good idea. Put on some of your favorite clothes and enjoy your night, yeah?"

Alex couldn't help but smile at him. Always adorable and helpful. "Yeah. I love you."

"Love you, too."

So, Alex did just that. They donned their favorite purple polka-dotted boxers, prosthetic packer, short sleeve button-up, and jet-black jeans, and reclined in their bed, hair up in a messy bun. They retrieved their writing notebook from the trenches of their dresser, and sat in silent contemplation. With what Ryan said at the top of their mind, hesitant at first but determined to finish, they wrote the following poem:

FtM

Another morning, another gender identity crisis.

What gender am I?

I am at once
"this guy," "that girl,"
"he," "they,"
"that genderless person."

"What are your pronouns?"
"What does genderfluid even mean?"
Imagine those questions
from the mouths of strangers.

Am I politically correct?
Am I legal?
A solemn, "no," scuttles its way across my eyes
as I imagine strangers shooting disgusted looks at me

in public.

In secrecy, I push down my chest
I strap on the prosthetic
switch out the light and stride out of the closet
to the edges of my bedroom
*not **she** or **he**.*

*I am **they**.*

Breaking the binary with careful snaps,
it crumbles between trembling, sweating fingers,
nails bitten down to the skin.

What if I don't subscribe to your preconceived notions
of gender or transgender?

Invalidation stems from people who say,
"You can be transgender, but only the right way."

***

Alex heard the words again. "I mean, you're not *dressed*," Ryan repeated in hushed tones, then hissed, "Get out of here, now! Before the principal…"

And then Principal Hatchett. "Miss Cesario! My office, young lady."

In a toppling domino effect, every face in the corridor flickered toward Alex as they found themselves smack-dab in the middle of the school in the "wrong" clothes.

CHAPTER 8

Across the foggy haze of the late fall afternoon, visible through the principal's office window, Alex would have thought the trees were on fire if they did not know better. *Well, maybe not on fire. They look like they're smoking, and at the heart of it all is a gaping charcoal maw consuming them from the inside.*

A smoking gun.

Alex blinked a few times to check themselves, and soon realized the dying trees weren't smoking at all, and neither were their leaves; they would smell it if they were. They loved that smell. The fogginess of both the day and of Alex's checked-out mind didn't help their delirium.

Alex could hear the distant echo of Principal Hatchett's admonishment. "Alexandra, I'm very disappointed in you. Do you know what you've done? Do you have the slightest clue of how much trouble you're facing? I'm calling your parents right now. Do you hear me? You have to be dealt with immediately. The proper protocols must be followed…" His droning was just as foggy in Alex's ears as those trees were in their mind. They vaguely registered the beeping of their principal dialing his private line, speaking a few short, halted sentences, then hanging up and whipping out a packet of paperwork and Alex's school record so fast they thought he was going to cut himself across his palms.

Alex shook off their doziness and came to, just in time to hear him say, "Alexandra, we need to start this paperwork. This," and he pushed a paper in front of Alex on FPNG letterhead with an official red insignia at the bottom, "is the Foundation for the Protection of Normative Gender's Gender Variance Charge Designation form. I don't like doing this, but you *need* to tell me… I *need* to report this. Why did you come to school dressed like, well," and Hatchett fumbled for the right words, "well, like *that* when your ID's gender designation is female?"

"I don't know." At least they were honest.

"Alexandra? I need you to answer truthfully."

"I am telling you the truth."

"Well, I cannot put 'I don't know' on this form, so please explain. In detail. I know you don't want to, but you must."

Alex desperately tried to sift through the muck of their situation, but all they felt was a resolute emptiness diametrically opposed to their roiling nerves, as if they were treading water. What was the point of this? Of anything? *Can I even be salvaged at this point?* "What happens next?" they queried, ignoring his question.

Principal Hatchett sighed and ran his meaty hand down the length of his clean-cut face. "Next, your parents arrive at school, I explain the situation, we submit a therapist request form, and you or your parents pay the requisite fine for breaking the law."

"How much is it?"

"Considering you were found and immediately detained before you could cause a ruckus? A thousand dollars, I wager."

"What?" Alex snapped out of their depressive fog. "What if my parents can't pay?"

"They can set up a payment plan. But first, I need you to cooperate and to explain how you ended up at school in *that*." He gave Alex another repulsed look that made their skin crawl. "And then you sign on the dotted line indicating you will never commit this transgression again or risk facing prison time. Understand?"

"Yes, I understand." Finally feeling the full weight of their current predicament, Alex obliged and calmly, voice trembling, lied to Principal Hatchett: They spun a tale of how, the week before, they found some "guy's" clothing in a donation bin near the school; they'd washed them and decided to try them on. They had intended to change out of the clothes and throw them back in the bin, but they'd fallen asleep after a long night of studying. Alex had briefly considered saying they'd borrowed the clothes, but even worse than facing punishment would be implicating someone else. Alex certainly was not going to out Ryan for secretly buying them clothes for months now.

As they signed and dated the statement, Alex's parents arrived and the school secretary swiftly shut the door behind them. After briefing Mr. and Mrs. Cesario of the situation, Principal Hatchett asked,

"Did you two know about this? Any clue at all?" Alex genuinely had no idea what they would say.

Alex's mum's fierce glare in their direction matched the principal's. Alex's dad gave them a soft, pitying look and lied. "No, we had no idea. Believe us, we're as shocked as you are." To make the point, Alex's mum feigned – or maybe not – a semi-disgusted look at them before turning back to the principal. Alex was sure she was faking, right? Or maybe she actually was disgusted. Or hurt and disappointed. Or maybe all of those things.

Principal Hatchett seemed satisfied by their answer. The last thing he needed, Alex supposed, was a conspiracy that he had failed to detect. In that case, he'd be culpable, too.

Why does nonbinary gender have to be this big cover-up? The FPNG's origins were as murky to Alex as anyone. The institution had been around since long before Alex was born, hell, probably before their parents. Not that their parents would talk of such things. Mrs. and Mr. Cesario loved and supported Alex as much as they could, but there were boundaries not to be crossed, even with them.

The smoky fog of the dead tree branches diverted Alex's attention once again, and they distanced themselves. *What now?* They thought they heard their mum scribbling on a piece of paper, perhaps signing the section at the end of the Gender Variance Charge Designation form that committed them to ensuring Alex religiously stuck to the binary gender coding upheld by the law.

They vaguely registered their parents' commitment to paying the outlined fine, and Alex was scheduled for a series of appointments with an after-school counselor under Principal Hatchett's supervision.

Finally, the principal uttered gruff words of satisfaction. "All right, we should be all set here. You'll receive an official statement in the mail and a copy of this form for your records once I mail it to the Foundation. Additionally, they'll send you a follow-up contract which you, Alexandra, and three other family members must sign, verifying her future compliance. In the meantime, please take Alexandra home and see that she changes into proper attire."

"We will," Alex's parents agreed in unison.

***

A week later, Alex and Jo waited to board a crowded flight to Seattle. Alex passed the time chatting with Ryan on the phone, sighing in resignation. "Well, at least I get to escape Springfield for a little bit, even if it's just for Thanksgiving break. I wish you could come too, Ryan."

"Believe me, I feel the same. You need someone to keep an eye on you." The wink inherent in his statement was not lost on Alex. "But the fam wants me here, so here is where I'll be when you get back."

"I told you they put me in counseling, right? Well, *forced* is more the word for it. Now, three days a week, I have to spend an hour after school convincing a therapist that I'm a female or woman or whatever, and that I identify as such and didn't know what I was doing, blah blah blah."

"You know your parents didn't have a choice." *You got me there*, Alex thought. "I'm surprised they're letting you go on this trip."

"I'm surprised the FPNG is letting me go on this trip. My parents were ready to kill me when we got home. 'You promised you'd be careful,' my mum kept repeating, and my dad just looked resigned. Talk about having your heart gutted. That's what it must feel like."

"So, they're fine with it all?"

"Yeah, right." Alex almost spat into the phone with all the venom in their voice. "They're hellfire mad at me. The money's going to be tough, too. The only reason they're allowing Jo and I to still go is because the tickets are non-refundable. The shitty thing is that they know I didn't do it on purpose."

Ryan sighed. "Yeah, at first, I wondered. I hate to say it, but the way you were talking that one night…"

"But I wouldn't have done it."

"When it came down to it, I know you wouldn't have self-sabotaged, but the whole thing's still scary. Are you grounded for life? Are your parents blaming me?"

"No, they're not blaming you. And yes, grounded indefinitely for my own safety, they said. I'm not sure I believe them. I don't know what to believe. I certainly don't believe in myself." Alex slumped their shoulders. "Anyway, we'd saved up for this flight for a while, so my parents wanted Jo and I to still get to see our aunt. My last flight of freedom, I wager."

Over the intercom, Alex heard, "Attention passengers, now boarding United Flight 495. Passengers seated in Zone D may board at this time."

"Shit, we gotta board in a minute. You want to meet me at the airport on Saturday afternoon?" Alex asked.

"Sure! You know I'd love to."

Jo's calm voice cut in. "Alex, we have to go." She leaned over across their lap and into Alex's cell phone speaker. "Bye, Ryan!"

"Geez, give a guy time to say goodbye to his best friend first. Bye Alex, stay safe."

"I will. Be here when I get back?"

"Absolutely."

CHAPTER 9

Ryan's promise to "absolutely be there" when Alex disembarked was the only thought drawing them from the cabin of their return flight and through the long, plain, gray-carpeted corridor that led into the Springfield International Airport's Domestic Arrival Terminal.

Inside Alex's earbuds, Bastille's lead singer, Dan Smith, sang a sarcastic ode in punchy phrasing about armchair warriors who lounge on their couches, aimlessly flicking through TV channels in an attempt to remove themselves from society's wider horrors while chaos reigns around them.

"Do you want to be free of this?" he asks of a world where real life feels like more like hell than fiction.

Am I sleepwalking through life, too? Alex wondered.

Yanking their earbuds out by the string, Alex begged Jo to stop at the terminal's Starbucks to grab a caramel macchiato and delay their inevitable return to the trenches of daily life in Springfield. They only had one day of buffer between them and the rest of the fall term, and the thought sickened Alex, churning their stomach. The call out from Principal Hatchett was a betrayal. Alex used to love school, the pure academia anyway, but now more than ever, school was just another battlefield. The fines, the therapy, the threats of legal removal from the city – Alex was well versed in the consequences of their existence from the vile FPNG flyers all over the city. Though Alex certainly feared capture, the concept used to be a distant improbability. Those empty threats were once just words. Now they were very real.

Sure, it's all theory and conjecture until those threats hail you back into society, into your place, into your lived reality as just another cog in the greater machine.

Unfortunately, as Jo reminded Alex, both cheerily and forcefully, their parents and Ryan were waiting for them outside the terminal. They couldn't hide in the airport forever.

"Why not?" Alex replied. "There's food, emergency beds, an ATM, and it's open twenty-four hours. It's the perfect hideout. With

flights flitting in and out at all hours, they can't shut this place down."
The liminality of Springfield Airport struck Alex in that moment. The
airport's very existence was predicated on people coming and going,
staying just for a short while. Even those who worked there went home
at the end of their shifts.

Apart from Ryan and their family, Alex felt no one besides
the police and the FPNG wanted them, so the airport seemed like a
momentary save haven.

"Let's go, slowpoke." Jo's perky voice pulled Alex back into
reality, into the day, into the task at hand: leaving the airport. Simple
enough for any cisgender person who followed the rules. Over their
vacation in the Pacific Northwest, Alex had behaved themselves,
following all of those pesky rules. All female all the time, as Ryan had
said when Alex called him to check in on Thanksgiving Day.

"All right, all right," they replied begrudgingly.

Sterile corridor after sterile corridor, Alex and Jo wound their
way through the airport, back toward their regular lives. Bypassing the
tempting food court, they approached the terminal's all-glass atrium
with swaths of charter and shuttle buses, taxis, and cars dotting the
sidewalk outside, when Alex noted a crew of three black-cloaked,
armed officials walking their way. Alex tried to read their hats to see
if they were FPNG; it wasn't out of the ordinary to see them patrolling
transportation hubs.

The officers were about to eclipse them – Alex *swore* their
trajectory was going past them, their sights set on another victim.
But then they abruptly halted right in front of Alex and Jo, blocking
them from their family and Ryan, who they could now see just beyond
security, waving.

"Oh, sorry. Excuse us." Jo took Alex's hand and tried to steer
them away from the three officers, certain they would be pissed if two
teens got in their way in the middle of important business.

The frontmost officer motioned for them to stop with an
outstretched hand. "Alexandra Victoria Cesario?"

"Y…Yes?" Alex stammered. "Why?" Their stomach dropped,
a clammy sweat spreading across their lower back.

"ID, please."

Fingers fumbling, Alex dug out their ID from their skirt's pocket and handed it over to the officer, still trembling. Lifting up his sunglasses, he read it, nodded at his companions, and produced a set of handcuffs. Jo's grip on Alex's wrist grew tighter.

"Alexandra Cesario, you are under arrest for…" The rest of his sentence faded into the void as Alex's focus went fuzzy, scrambling for comprehension. The words were unreal. They couldn't be. The FPNG, here for them? No way. Impossible. Alex watched the scene unfold as if standing ten feet away from their body, unable to grasp what was happening.

As if he was speaking underwater, the words filtered in. "…for violating the aforementioned guidelines set forth by the Foundation for the Protection of Normative Gender. Having received proper warning and notice…"

They were cognizant of screams from beyond the security barrier, and as the official locked Alex's wrists in his cuffs, they locked eyes with their hysterical mum and dad. One of the other lackeys restrained Jo, who was kicking and screaming to get back to Alex. Immobilized with disbelief and fear, Alex thought their parents might faint by the looks of them, but they could barely see anything through their bleary and tear-stained eyes.

"… and as a repeat offender, we have no choice but to arrest you."

Ryan launched himself over the barrier and sprinted at Alex, but a loud siren sounded from the security station and all he could do before the officers seized him was briefly brush Alex's cheek with his thumb, taking some of their tears with him. Seeing Ryan restrained devastated Alex, as they realized they wouldn't be able to live without him. Alex felt their heart crack open from the tragedy of it all.

A choking sob broke Ryan's voice as he screamed, "Alex! We'll get you back! You'll come back!" Alex could only manage a low, aching, heart-wrenching sob in return.

"Anything you say can and will be used against you…"

Sirens blared from outside, and Alex was dragged and shoved into the back of a cold, armored van. The officer locked Alex's cuffs to a ring in the wall, and the last thing they heard before the door slammed in their face was, "Take them to the Northeast Panoptic."

Slam!

Darkness.

Alex heard something else shift in that darkness, a wet cough and a tentative voice.

Wait, that officer said they. *He wouldn't have used that pronoun for me. Is there someone else here with me? I was so disoriented, blinded by the sun, I didn't notice.*

"Alex?"

The voice was unmistakable. How could Alex forget anyone from the quashed nonbinary meeting that awful night?

"Xavier?"

"The bedrock of the Foundation is beginning to crumble," was Xavier's monotone, whispered reply.

CHAPTER 10

For many, dark and stormy nights signal trouble and damnation: the rainy gloom with pattering rain droplets accompanying the constant tick of a grandfather clock; the aroma of mist-drowned leaves and the smell of fall; the sound of Halloween trick-or-treaters plodding along the sidewalk, their laughter and screams filling the heavy air. Alex reveled in those sensations, and in the pinpricks of orange and yellow streetlights bleeding into the thick fog around them.

Those nights that bundled Alex in their secure, spooky ambience had nothing on the beastly, stark, unfriendly sun of this late November day, piercing its finger down on Alex as FPNG officials shoved them into an armored van in broad daylight. *Do they capture us in public to make an example of us?*

Alex tried to make sense of what had happened, but it was all too murky. Xavier said something in the darkness.

"What was that?"

Xavier repeated his whisper. "The bedrock of the Foundation is beginning to crumble. Alex, the system."

Still spun in the hysteria of their arrest, eyes bulging in shock, Alex asked in a crazed voice, "Where are the others?" Their mind was still back in that airport. If given a do-over, Alex would have never left Seattle. *But would they have sought me out there, too? Would I have been arrested regardless of where I hid, and extradited back to Springfield? Would the state boundaries have made any difference?*

"Shay? Where is she? Have you seen her? Dakota? Riley? Skyler? Any of them?" Alex persisted, their mind wild and unable to focus.

Xavier sighed, recognizing that he wasn't going to get through to them. "Alex, look," he paused, hesitant to share bad news. "I don't know where the others are. After that awful meeting, we all scattered, just like you and Ryan did. I know they grabbed Shay, for sure. I managed to get away, but…" and he shook his shackled hands behind his back to make his point.

"Not even Dakota?"

"Nope. I saw ze a week or so later, but since then, it's been radio silence. At first, I thought it was me. We… we were kind of starting to date. But now that you mention it, I wonder if something's wrong."

Three heavy bangs from the front of the van interrupted Alex. "No talking! Keep quiet back there. We're en route to the station."

"Station?" whispered Alex.

"No clue."

Not knowing where they were being taken made Alex feel crazy, vulnerable, out of control. They knew that they'd be transported to the Northeast Panoptic, or at least, that's what the officer had said, but where was that, exactly? Alex presumed the Panoptic would be up in the mountains somewhere, but that was mere conjecture. The Panoptica had to be remote, removed from regular society, ever the unseen, ominous threat. How would the FPNG transport them to the Panoptic? Was there a rendezvous point outside the city?

Fifteen minutes later, Alex and Xavier slammed into the van's icy walls as it came to a halt. The guards yanked them out of the back, and Alex realized that their quiet assumption of landing in the city outskirts had been way off-base. They blinked in the harsh sunlight and looked up at the towering skyscrapers; they were still in the heart of Springfield, parked on an access road behind Springfield's South Station.

"In with ya, come on, let's go!"

They stumbled into the gloom of the station, the guards nearly stepping on their heels for how close they were, one tight fist constricting Alex's right wrist, which was still cuffed to their left. *Never been in this section of South Station before. Looks like the basement or some derelict part left over from the original building.* They weren't sure why, but they knew it was important to take stock of every place they went, every part of the process, should there be a chance to escape. *Not that that's likely.*

The platform looked abandoned, forgotten, and Alex couldn't make out anyone but the four of them, eyes bleary from the stark transition from midday sunlight to the dungeon-like dais. Forward they forged into the den, disoriented, and what Alex had assumed to be the far brick wall of the platform turned out to be a train, rusting in several places, including the body and wheels. The evident neglect struck a chord with them. Are *we getting on this thing? Surely, it's not safe. Recycled from who knows where.*

Xavier was pulled toward a different cart closer to the engine. "I'll come find you!" he called out before being thrust up a small set of stairs and into the ancient train.

"Yeah, that's not going to happen," scoffed the guard holding Alex. "All right miss, you're off to the ladies' end of the train."

"We're separated by gender here, too?"

"Oh, yes."

Alex was forced into the decrepit cart, lined on both sides with slim doors that led to even slimmer compartments. Cells. They were uncuffed and shoved into one of their own, which was barely big enough for two people to stand in.

Each compartment featured a cushioned bench, faded and nearly flat, and a toilet. *Only the finest facilities. I wonder how long this is going to take.* The officer departed, and for the first moment since they left Seattle, Alex was alone.

The train lurched forward in unsteady chugs half an hour later, and it knocked Alex back onto the tight floorspace; thus, their journey somewhere north began. From their narrow compartment window, they saw clumps of steam puff upward into the darkness, physical evidence of the long, huffing sighs of the train as it dragged the carts forward with slow momentum. Once it picked up speed, Alex leaned their head against the cold inner wall, relishing the quiet, steady *thrumm* of the train.

***

Several hours passed and Alex awoke feeling short of breath but unaware of the cause. The distinct residue of a dream clung to the edges of their mind, but damned if they could remember what it was just a few seconds later. It felt happy, whatever it was, which made waking with a gasp all the more unwelcome.

Get your breathing under control, Alex reminded themselves. *Panicking won't do a thing but make this situation worse. Regulate your body. Mindfulness. In... out...*

A full minute later, Alex held their breathing steady, and stepped up onto their rickety bench to look out the window, searching for a landmark or clue to their location. They saw nothing but an expanse of azure sky rising above a low rim of wispy clouds. The tempo of the train was slow, sluggish but steady. Despite their circumstances, Alex remarked at the stark, sublime, simple beauty of the sight, then wondered where the heck they were.

What altitude is this? I can't see anything but sky and clouds. Maybe that's why it was so hard to breathe when they woke; if the altitude changed, that would certainly explain things.

A mountain? Was I correct? Alex wondered, and the train hitched to a stop. A cold sweat sprung from the pores on their back. *Are we here? Where's here? What will the next moment bring? What will happen when we disembark?* In this moment, even with all its writhing and panic, an unknown energy struck Alex, as surreal and sublime as the landscape around them.

Screeeeeech. All the cart's compartment doors scraped open at once, allowing a blinding white light to reflect off the entirely metal interior of the train car. An errant ray darted into Alex's eye and they shielded themselves with an arm.

"Everyone out!" an authoritative voice commanded, and a bitter, cutting wind penetrated the innards of their train car. With heavy reluctance, they stepped down from the bench and peeked their head outside the door, seeing ten other faces do the same. A stark, black silhouette framed their exit, waving them forward with a nightstick. Fearing the consequences of staying put, Alex was among the first to step out, the wide eyes of the others following them as they hopped out of the car and onto the solid, frosted ground.

In a breathy exhale, Alex thought, *I was right after all. The mountains.* Not only was Alex plum in the middle of the White Mountains, but they were on the highest peak in the region: Mount Washington. They remembered the view from the "Best of the Northeast" tourist brochures that littered many of the coastal restaurants and gift shops, once a real attraction but now relegated to the likes of a Stock image to beautify the attractive pamphlets. Pedestrian travel up the mountain was strictly forbidden, as the peak was too dangerous for amateurs. Thus, the once-famous Cog Railroad and Mount Washington Auto Road had been disengaged.

So, this is where they hid it. The whipped summits surrounding the rocky pedestal on which they stood looked akin to a freshly fired Baked Alaska. The expansive beauty of the scene was vastly different than the microcosmic view Alex had from their measly train window. No, this was something altogether more moving, more powerful, and all the more frightening for it. Alex flashed back to English class just a month before, and the view conjured a primal rendition of Percy Bysshe Shelley's poem, "Mont Blanc." Unlike the mountain represented in Shelley's stanzas, Alex doubted that Mount Washington had the supreme power to erase the harmful scriptures that originate from hate, envy, and woe.

The train continued to idle, perched at a ramshackle station at the summit. Looking downward, Alex noticed the row of winding tracks that climbed up the mountainous tundra in a circumference around the Northeast Panoptic behind them, so the trains could then descend on the same track. One track in, one track out.

That's both convenient and prohibitive. On the one hand, there's no way a stray car could scale the tracks, but on the other, if a rockslide or a blizzard takes the tracks out, we'd be stuck, even the guards. The weather on this mountain is more erratic than any other on the northeastern coast.

As the remaining detainees poured out of the train, Alex noticed they were mostly teens, maybe one or two college-aged kids. All young people, just trying to be themselves in this world. They searched desperately for Xavier, for anyone they recognized, but found none. The guards ushered them toward the prison-like building; they would soon be out of the whipping, howling winds that slid across the summit.

Here sat the Northeast Panoptic: a sulking, cylindrical brick building, devoid of wide windows except for a small, neat row near the base. *The guards' quarters and offices,* thought Alex. Small slits ran in circles around its hulking mass, ring after ring scaling two stories, they supposed. *Prison cell windows?* Atop the Panoptic sat a squat dome roof with massive, heavy shingles weighing it down. The tower was built from what Alex presumed was once white brick, now gray and weathered. A light dusting of snow from the morning adorned everything in sight except the train. A small outbuilding, resembling the Panoptic in miniature, stood separately off to the left, dangerously close to the cliffside. *The summit's weather station, perhaps.*

"In lines of two!" barked an officer from behind, and Alex and their peers all filed away from the train and shivered against the chill. They stood no chance of surviving the summit's harsh weather alone or on foot. "One line for boys, one line for girls." *Of course.*

The group marched inside, dutifully in their gender-segregated lines, under the watchful eyes of guards. The bare front lobby held nothing but another guard at a desk stacked high with file folders, intake paperwork, and records. File cabinets filled the remainder of the space, running almost as high as the ceiling. Corridors to the left and right of the entrance led to unmarked areas, and as the officers directed the girls' line to the right and the boys' to the left, another shiver wracked Alex's body as they tried to anticipate what was to come.

As the girls arrived at their designated room, a man aptly named Officer Paine handed each inmate a thin stack of black clothing: a simple V-neck shirt, pants, skirt, and slip-on shoes. Alex and their peers were ordered to change into these clothes under the watch of a guard the FPNG would categorize as female, after which, Officer Paine returned and instructed them to sit on long wooden benches until called by name.

Alex watched as five people were called and led through a barred doorway at the far end of the bleak room; Paine waved his access card across the door's scanner to open it for every new person. Finally, it was their turn to meet their fate. "Cesario, Alexandra!"

Alex offered a timid wave and Paine's index finger beckoned them forward. He roughly gripped their right arm as they approached.

"I've got the next one here, sir," Officer Paine addressed his superior at the barred door's threshold.

"Great," the disembodied voice said. "Put her in our next open cell on the second floor. How many are left to be processed?"

"Twenty or so, sir."

"We should be able to accommodate that. But we're almost at capacity here. The cells are filling fast. Officer Paine?"

"Yes, sir?"

"Report to the Communications Tower directly after this young lady…"

There was that awful phrase again. Alex cringed and shrunk their shoulders at the words, "young lady," their ear drums bursting with discomfort as if Officer Paine had scraped his nails along a chalkboard. It's just the worst.

"… is in her cell. Tell the Comm. Associate to redirect any future incoming prisoners to the other regional Panoptica until next week."

"Yes, sir." After a salute from Officer Paine, they were off.

Filling up? Alex thought. *How many poor folks are trapped here?* Paine shoved them forward and into the mire.

The transfer from the processing chamber to Alex's cell was brief: off to the left and up a steep, rickety metal flight of stairs that was so narrow Alex could barely fit, they saw the Northeast Panoptic's main atrium in all its faded glory. The cavernous interior featured a shallow dome ceiling. A thin watchtower stood in the very center of the space, surrounded on all sides by two stories of prison cells. From their vantage, Alex surmised that the glass windows that enclosed the watchtower were designed to allow the guards to monitor the prisoners from any angle, day and night. With only skinny stairways and thin, cement walkways connecting the cells to one another and the level below, any escape attempt would be instantly spotted by the guards in the tower.

As they were escorted around the perimeter, Alex caught intermittent clips of movement out of the corner of their eye. They realized the watchtower wasn't built from glass, but from pristine mirrors. The movement they noticed was their own reflection.

Why the mirrors? What were their purpose?

CHAPTER 11

Self-reflection – that is the purpose of the mirrors, realized Alex after two long days had slipped by. *That's so stupidly blatant. Are they supposed to have an impact? Are they supposed to make us feel something? It seems like the point would be more forcefully made if mirrors were hung around each cell. I hate to look at my body in certain lights and certain clothing. I suspect that the reason they're out there is for safety; they can't have inmates getting self-destructive ideas or attacking officers. I'm not tempted, but I know others who might be.*

***

What does it mean to be nonbinary? Alex thought in the still quiet of that afternoon, picking at a few errant chin hairs and staring into the blank nothingness of their cell ceiling. *I don't have to look one way or another, manifest my gender one way or another, or be on a certain set of hormones. I'm nonbinary in and of myself, much like Kieran.*

Kieran...

But unlike Kieran, I'm uncomfortable with my body as it is. It's not that there is anything wrong with my body; being assigned female at birth wasn't a cage in childhood, wasn't the curse that others feel. Hell, I love certain parts of my body: my arms, my legs, my slight peach fuzz – all genetics. Nonetheless, there are certain parts I would love to change.

All the time I've had to myself, nothing but endless time to think, has led me to this realization. All the small, creeping thoughts I've shot down for almost a decade, since the start of puberty, were never really gone. Little did I know they were piling up all the while, and there's no windbreak in sight.

I like my body, but I don't like my hips, my period, my high-pitched voice, my genitals. I want to alter these parts of my body to become more of the person I truly am. Hormone replacement therapy is what I want. HRT will not make me a guy, male, a man, or whatever you call cisgender people with testosterone as the primary hormone in their bodies. Even considering all this, I am still nonbinary.

I am not a man or a woman, lady or dude. I live and love outside those limiting strictures. At least, I would like to live outside those strictures. Trying my best to be myself within the confines of the law wound me up here.

Could I ever imagine people calling me sir or he? Why does penis plus low voice plus facial hair equal male or guy? Why must we be that restrictive? Can't a person have those things and not be a guy? Why can't someone have those things and be a girl or feminine-presenting? Or neither? Or both?

How are these stringent limitations helpful? To whom are they helpful?

They're only indicative of a systematic desire to uphold a long-outdated status quo.

Can we reinvent the status quo?

I love to imagine another place, another lifetime in which I can go out in public as myself, as Alex and not as Alexandra, or who everyone assumes Alexandra is based on how I dress. In this place, my reflexes would not be tuned to shrinking back from people in public, from resisting mentioning being genderfluid and nonbinary. The impulse then wouldn't be to shamefully hide myself, but rather, to be proud of who I am and what my journey to self-realization represents. Could such a time and place exist, in the future, perhaps? As far as I can tell, all of the United States, from Portland to Springfield, is set up with these same gender-restrictive standards. Even the far-flung reaches of society, from those living high in the mountain crags of the Rockies to those on isolated farm estates in northern Maine, are held to the same FPNG expectations. No matter how far I run, I cannot completely escape. Even those remote farmers have to socialize occasionally to make their living, to continue their remote existence.

In this alternate existence, I'd walk hand in hand with Kieran into the only gay (read: queer) club in downtown Ogunquit, the randomly queer coastal seaside town near York. We'd chat with the other locals at the dimly lit bar with rainbow uplighting, then move to the dance floor when our awkward fumbling of adolescent affection felt smoother, greased with the confidence that only a young, invincible, alcoholic daze can foster. I'd punctuate that ideal picture with definitive strokes of a sign reading, "All-Gender Restroom," including both stalls and urinals. What if such a radical place could exist? I'd do anything to rally and make that dream a reality, even commonplace. But what can I do about that impossible future now?

Can anything be done? Any action taken? Not from inside this cell, that's for sure.

No matter how I feel about Kieran now, I love that they love their body as it is and embrace it. I envy that.

I envy Ryan, as well. I know he's nonbinary through and through, but he successfully walks the binary tightrope every day for the sake of public presentation. He knew who he was, he knew how to align his body with who he is, and he went for it. You can never fault someone for having the courage to do that.

I could never imagine not being gender variant, to identify within a fragile, glass-castle-constructed gender binary.

How does one manage to "be binary?"

Would I rather have been born a cisgender man? Ryan's asked me that once or twice, because the body image I'm searching for is similar to how FPNG "men" present. I'm still unsure about how to answer that. Today, I'd answer "yes," which I think is sad. Maybe that answer will change someday.

What is it to be a "man" or a "woman?" Sure, those genders are set legally by societal standards and the law that says every person should be assigned a gender. But apart from a designation on an ID card, a license, a birth certificate, a student's permanent record, when we interrogate the core of the issue, what kinds of people do those terms really describe? What is a "man" or a "woman" or a person outside of the FPNG's definition? When one says "woman" or "man," a set of images, expectations, and characteristics come to mind: vagina or penis, a certain style of clothing, generally short or long hair, personality characteristics, and behavioral expectations.

Our ancestors set those expectations and binaries, those boxes, those restrictions.

105

I wish gender weren't such a restriction. I wish that there were flexibility in it.

Along those same lines, what does it mean to be "feminine" or "masculine?" It's rare that people will accept you if you are both; there is always the obligation to be one or the other. Feminine or masculine, one set of gender expectations or the other. If we strip away other people's expectations of femininity and masculinity – not only those set by the wider world but also those perpetuated by our parents, relatives, and friends, perhaps unknowingly – what do those words mean anyway? What would it mean to be masculine or feminine in one's own right, absent of others' expectations? When we wipe away all previously established meaning, what's left? Imagine a world so free and so accepting that we could live out our own expectations of masculinity and femininity, neither or both, regardless of genitals, assigned gender, and sexual orientation.

Today, femininity and masculinity aren't freeing, they're restrictive. What is freedom of expression? What if femininity and masculinity weren't so rigid? What if we could define those terms and their parameters for ourselves?

Imagine being able to be nonbinary and masculine and feminine, as one defines oneself and one's identity. Would chaos erupt with the destruction of binaries? What would it mean for those who look to categories for definition, identification, and validation? Would it be right to eliminate them entirely?

What would a post-binary society look like? Free?

For me, being nonbinary means living my truth. But when living your truth results in isolation, socially and physically, enforced by a system that preys on that isolation, what then?

Will nonbinary and gender variant individuals always be stamped social outcasts? Is social change possible? I believe that it's possible with a catalyst if we make it possible. How are we, as nonbinary people, to do that when we can't speak up, when we can't be ourselves, when our voices and opinions and lives are squashed?

Damn, they thought, *maybe those tower mirrors do have a discernable effect after all.*

Being a nonbinary person means living outside the constituted norm, a norm threaded into the very fabric from which our infrastructure and social systems were built. Binary gender structures are too limiting.

Alex chuckled to themselves, cynically taking stock of their situation, of their bare body in a standard-issue uniform, of their bare cell. *Literally limiting. I don't see the cisgender and binary trans people of the world doing much to change that, not here, not in a world in which the Panoptica exist and the FPNG prey on individuals such as ourselves.*

Why? They don't want to surrender their "approved" status, that little green stamp that says, "I am legal. I am accepted. I am safe." To surrender those rights is to abandon their safety net; why would anyone do that? If I were cis or binary, would I do that? Would I make such a sacrifice for strangers? Considering my current state, probably not.

A brutal thought struck Alex as they reflected on approval and privilege, especially the relative privilege of binary people in relation to those who are not, and the status that such a privilege grants them. *Hey, at least I get a single stall, ungendered bathroom while I'm here. How pathetic is that? It takes incarceration to use an ungendered bathroom that's not in somebody's house. Sure, there are probing eyes everywhere: the guards circling like scavengers, in the watchtower, even myself when I catch a slanted, blurry image of myself reflected back from the watchtower mirrors. But at least I don't have to endure the probing eyes of other women and feminine-presenting people in the restroom. Even when I wore the "correct" clothing, I still felt self-conscious.*

Would Juneau do anything to change our system? Where is she? I hope she's in better condition than I am.

"Inmate 2331! Dinner time."

2331. Am I only the 2331st prisoner to be shoved through these gates? Or do they reuse numbers as they "reform" us and new prisoners are exchanged for old? Alex reluctantly swung themselves into a sitting position. They glanced out the thin window at the top of their cell wall, across from their door to the Panoptic's outer atrium.

107

Slim slivers of dull silver clouds drifted across a bruised burgundy sky. Alex noticed that the fluffy clouds' underbellies wore a skirt of deep gold, the remainder of the day's sunshine manifesting on their bodies, paling as the moments passed, the sun spread thin, and the sky sunk into darkness, dampening the brief respite of the scene.

"Yup," was Alex's exhausted reply. They heard the long *beeeep* and *ch-lick* as a guard swiped their access card to open Alex's cell and deliver their meal. Lost in their mindless daze, Alex didn't register the name of the anonymous guard, until, with a few hard blinks, they refocused enough to read the block lettering stitched onto the guard's left shirt sleeve: J. ANDERSON.

Alex could barely believe that the person in the FPNG uniform before of them had Juneau's kind eyes, but a sad and soft expression.

"Alex?" she whispered, and Alex's eye darted to meet her, a slight tremble in the guard's hands as she placed the food tray at the foot of Alex's bed.

"Juneau?"

CHAPTER 12

"J... Juneau? Who are you? You can't be..." *She* would *be here. I mean, I assumed she was here. But as a guard?*

Juneau continued. "Alex. Alex, what are you doing here?"

"Isn't it obvious? I got arrested."

"Why?"

"Again, obvious."

"Yeah, but who could have..."

Alex cut her off. "Dunno. It could have been Kieran or their uncle, for all I know."

"Kieran?"

"Uhh..."

"We can talk later. I need to go, but I'll be back."

Alex fired back, "I'll be here, clearly. Not going anywhere anytime soon." Again, those searching eyes from Juneau. Before she could return to the Panoptic's atrium and lock the cell door behind her, Alex said, "Is this where you've been the entire time?"

With heavy regret, Juneau replied, "Yes. I'll tell you more, just... not now."

"But aren't you dysphoric as hell?" Alex looked her up and down and couldn't recognize the guard standing above them, still rocked with disbelief and desperate to keep her here a few moments longer. "Dressed like this? This isn't you. I see someone else right now. Is this really where you've been the entire time? All these months? We've been so worried."

"Ha, I bet. But yes, it is a bit dysphoric. Still, at the end of the day, I'm still me. These clothes are only temporary." She turned like she was going to leave, but then paused. "Wait, before I go, I have to ask..."

"Anything."

"How's Ryan?" Her tone was full of pain and longing, which also manifested in Juneau's expression. Alex smiled, knowing the love that the two friends have for one another, knowing that it is real, whatever the outcome.

"He's good, Juneau. Relatively behaved, as far as Ryan goes. But…"

"But what?"

"He was there when I got arrested." Alex dropped their eyes to the floor and scratched at the cold sweat accumulating on the back of their neck below their hairline. "I don't know what he's up to now. He didn't take it well."

"I see. I miss him, more than I can say. I've missed you, too."

"I bet. And I know. We've missed you desperately."

"You behave while you're here, okay?"

With that final suggestion, Juneau made an about-face and snuck out of Alex's cell, avoiding their look of consternation.

***

I'm running down the list of names, searching in desperate leaps and bounds to determine who could have possibly sold me out, but no one clear name comes to mind. Who knows that I'm nonbinary? In another life, another lifetime, making a list like this would be ludicrous, ticking off the names of who knows the real me and who doesn't, having to walk that careful tightrope.

Mum and dad. Jo. Everyone at the group from September, but they've either been captured or are in hiding, except for Ryan. Ryan, obviously. Kieran. Kieran's uncle. Now, the principal.

Could it have been Kieran's uncle? They assured me he was cool, but how do they know for sure? Would they bank their survival on it? My survival?

Back to my list: no one in my family could have betrayed me, I've concluded.

But what about Kieran? I keep fixating on them as a possible suspect. I had serious feelings for them, but I still don't know them that well. Or their uncle… Yeah, I bet their questionable uncle is the source of my demise. Or at the very least, the catalyst for it.

Or could Principal Hatchett have apprised my teachers of the situation? Could peaceable Mrs. Du Bois have become an informant? What about the waiter at La Bocca Forte? Whoever informed the FPNG of my variance matters little now. Sadly, the result is the same.

Why should I be held accountable? Why should I be blamed for my circumstances?

It's all these shitty people and their pathetically fragile societal forces who are to blame.

I'll completely miss out on Christmas Eve, won't I?

More momentous and important than Christmas Day itself, Alex recalled countless Christmas Eves spent at their grandparents' house in the country. Decorated to the brim with holly, thistle, red bows entwined with evergreen garland, faux white candles in every window, Sparkling Pine Yankee Candles burning in the center of every dinner table, the house was dressed to the nines. Alex's family would cobble together multiple tables in multiple rooms of the petite colonial, each relative trading seats with another as they made their way around the house to catch up with everyone and try to make up for lost time. And they wouldn't dare forget their grandfather's famous punch, which consisted of Hawaiian Punch, Tom Collins mix, lemon-lime soda, and seltzer, with scoops of rainbow sherbet floating on top. Somehow, that punch was more evocative of Christmas than the more traditional and boring eggnog.

They were getting older, so Alex feared they didn't have many of those Christmas Eves left with their grandparents and made a conscious effort to cherish each one of them.

What would Grandma and Grandpa think of me being nonbinary, of being transgender, never mind a nonbinary, genderfluid, transgender person? I can't even imagine what they would think, much less what they would say to my face. Grandma still sees me as her precious little girl, a child with wide eyes and a curious mind, an avid reader. Their heads would spin at the revelation.

But I'm no one's girl.

A product of their parents before them, my parents raised me in the close-knit, woven fabric of an Irish Catholic family. The traditional, intrinsic message instilled in my grandparents was that gay people were hated, damned to hell, that one should be ashamed if one was gay. I still don't know my grandparents' stance on trans people, but I sure do know what the Church thinks. Grandma and Grandpa don't "hate the gays" anymore, as the slogan was just a few short years ago, but they also lap up most of the saccharine bullshit that institutionalized religion feeds them, God-fearing as they are. "Love the sinner, hate the sin," and all of that nonsense. The Catholic Church isn't kind to trans people, never mind anyone who identifies as nonbinary or nonbinary and trans. The Pope can placate the general public and seem as "accepting" as he wants, but the culture he represents still pushes conversion therapy and other practices that actively harm and endanger trans lives across the world. With that context in mind, would my grandparents accept me? The question is gut-wrenching, and one I've never vocalized, not even to Ryan or to my parents. Presenting as I was, a "proper female," even thinking about it seemed useless.

Being trans is one thing, but pronouns are another consideration. Nowhere in my wildest dreams do I think my grandparents would use my pronouns; it's a far-flung impossibility. I can yammer about being trans and also nonbinary until the cows come home, but would they understand, accept, and embrace me? "Non-traditional" pronouns throw even the most "progressive," supposedly supportive, and LGBTQ-friendly people for a loop. No idea why. Pronouns are pronouns.

The year after my confirmation, my close friends helped me learn more about the Church's harmful practices, and I vowed to remove myself from it. I would only attend the occasional Christmas Eve mass – I enjoyed the organ music and the soaring choir – and important weddings and funerals. I informed my parents of my decision after one painfully dry and unfulfilling liturgy, conducted by the head priest who must have been older than the Church itself. They agreed it was my decision to make.

For a life in which many choices are beyond my reach, at least this decision was mine.

Other than the Christmas Eve mass music, the other aspect of church that I enjoyed was the antiquated majesty of the cathedral itself, especially the sun filtering in long shafts through the sky-high, stained glass windows, six on each side of the pews. Thinking of the particular way those windows made them feel, Alex was reminded of their occasional hikes outside the city at Walden Pond: lounging in the trees' shadows, the seemingly dusty, black tree boughs set in stark relief to the pond's azure water; the contrast evoking the church's thick, wooden window frames, the vibrant foliage of the leaves against the sun, stained glass simulacra in their own regard.

Komorebi.

The sublime feelings of peace inspired by both places were so intertwined that Alex seldom thought about one beauty without the other. The liminality of the pond and the stained glass windows was poignant to Alex: spaces between boundaries and binaries.

We could learn a thing or two about the serenity of the wilderness, uncharted as it sometimes is.

***

Juneau returned two days later with her story. Alex remembered the day specifically, amidst the blurring of the rest, because she arrived early with dinner while the sky remained a deep, lush, refreshing cerulean. The vibrant shade surprised Alex, given how late in the year it was and how dark they expected that time to look. They inched toward the winter solstice, each day shorter than the last.

"What took so long?" Alex felt their voice hitch in nervousness.

"Changing guard schedules; we rotate out. Plus, I can't be seen here, in your cell, for an inordinate amount of time. He'll think something is up."

"Who will?"

"Officer Paine, one of the more senior officers. Plus, I have others to check on and feed."

"Other prisoners like me?"

"Yes."

"Do you know where Xavier is? He's a friend of mine, and he arrived on the latest train with me."

"There's an Xavier right next door to you! At least, that's how he introduced himself. His birth name is something else." For a brief second, Alex wondered why the heck the guards would pay mind to Xavier's birth name, but then they remembered where they were. *Xavier can count himself lucky that he introduced himself as such to Juneau and not to another guard.*

Juneau leaned closer, and took on a hushed, conspiratorial tone, not that anyone could hear them with the cell door closed. But there's something about secrets – when we don't utter them in whispers, we still think others will hear us. "Also, your vent," she pointed to a small vent in the floor between Alex's bed and the stainless-steel toilet, "and Xavier's are connected. Every two cells share an air supply."

"Good to know." A petite smile pricked at the corners of Alex's mouth. With Juneau in the protective ranks and Xavier just next door, they no longer felt quite so desperately alone, both people offering a small sense of comfort. "Now, are you going to tell me how you got here, or not? I'm dying to know."

"Now that's the Alex I know: insistent, determined, and direct."

"And here I am, fallen from grace." The sarcasm rolled off Alex's tongue naturally. "Take a seat and tell me."

"I can't. I need to stand in sight of the guard tower at all times, strict orders."

Alex gestured their right wrist in circles, miming for Juneau to get on with it.

"All right, Alex, I'll humor you. Here's the story: You know that FPNG program that recruits kids after high school?"

"Unfortunately, yes. I tried to ignore it. Never was relevant to me."

"Well, that's what I joined. Basically, at the start of senior year, you sign up for an internship with the FPNG in addition to your full course load. There's an application, an essay, extensive background checks, the whole shebang. It's really a 'rock and a hard place' type of conundrum for them because they're strict about who they allow into the program, but they also need bodies in the field. That's why they try to recruit a plethora of folks before they get out of high school and have a chance to escape or resist the system. Your background must be spotless." She paused to sigh, admitting, "That's why I started to distance myself from Ryan and you guys. I couldn't risk anything, *wouldn't* risk my exposure. I hated doing it."

"We noticed. But then you outright disappeared." Alex attempted to compose their steely, unforgiving stare.

Juneau nodded. "I did. So, I applied, the FPNG accepted my application with little trouble, and I entered the FPNG training program. When you're not in school or with your family, you're in intensive training, even eight hours a day during the weekends. The strain on my parents was unreal, as was the stress on my personal freedom, or lack thereof."

"I'm so sorry. But why? Why did you willingly join them?"

"I had to do it, Alex. For you and for others like us." Juneau swiveled her head to the guard tower and back, double-checking that she was still in the clear. She smirked. "Me and a few others, friends of Shay's, we have a little group. Well, from what I hear, our group is not so little anymore.

"Once I completed the year, I was an officer-in-training. You know me and school stuff: once I set my mind to a goal, I fling everything I have at it. I passed, even exceeding the standings of other, more binary-minded cadets."

"But you disappeared sometime in early April, just after Easter. It was too early for graduation. You would have been there."

"I graduated early. I gained my instructors' steadfast trust and appreciation, and with their recommendation, I was assigned to be stationed here, at the Northeast Panoptic. I'm not the first to do so. We have about a dozen of us – people like you and I, but also a few allies – who've willingly made this sacrifice and have infiltrated the ranks over the years, waiting for the right moment, for the tipping point. Do you know Shay?"

"Ryan's Shay?" Alex asked. "Of course, she ran a nonbinary support group that I attended once."

"The very same. She was on track to follow in my footsteps, that is, until her capture. I doubt she ever thought she'd end up here as a prisoner."

115

"The FPNG caught up to her. I was there."

"She told me."

Gulp. Alex's guilt grabbed them by the throat and they could barely choke out, "She told you that Ryan and I left her behind? About that night?"

Stunned by Alex's reaction, Juneau assured, "What? Shay told me about the meeting, sure, and about the FPNG's assault, but she possesses no animosity toward you, Alex. Or Ryan. She hoped that you two escaped with a few others. She would never harbor any resentment; Shay's not that kind of person. She fights for survival."

Juneau's assurances did little to quell Alex's still-swelling guilt. Until they talked to Shay herself, they would remain unconvinced. Several questions nagged at Alex's brain, but the one they settled on was, "So, when's the tipping point?"

A wickedly fun smile danced across Juneau's face, ear to ear. "Soon."

"Why soon?"

"The Panoptic is at max capacity. There will be some pressure relief after the next round of 'reeducated' folks graduate, but after that, we'll be right back at capacity. It's been the same dance, over and over, for the entirety of my post here."

"I know, I overheard Officer Paine and some other guy…"

"Sheesh, the guards are getting careless. But it's true."

Lowering their voice to a whisper now, Alex went for the leap, a presumption of something radical. "Juneau, do you mean to say we're getting out of here? That you're breaking me – us – out? For good?"

"Yes, that's the plan in a nutshell."

"How? Why? There's a plan? Anything definite? When? What precautions have been taken? How can I help?" And then, without thinking, they wondered, "I can't imagine what Kieran would think of this."

"Hey hey, slow your roll, catch your breath. Kieran? I think I know that name, but I'm not sure how… At any rate, I'll tell you why: the Northeast Panoptic is the oldest in the system, and is seriously showing its age. As to how…" Juneau looked over her shoulder.

Alex suspected that their time was going to be cut short any moment. "Listen, Alex, I need to…"

"Peace out, I know. It's okay. Go. As long as you promise to come back. But how do you know Kieran?"

"More later. And you know I will." Juneau desperately wanted to offer a hug, but knew she couldn't.

As Juneau clicked the cell door shut, Alex felt surprisingly solemn, struck by the notion that if Juneau and her group weren't there to help them escape from the Northeast Panoptic, they wouldn't have been able to do to themselves.

How big a difference can one person make?

Is one person enough to become an entire movement's change agent?

Left with some solid time to reflect on Juneau's sudden reappearance in their life, Alex's next thought pivoted to Ryan. *How would Ryan react to the news about Juneau being alive? We didn't think she was dead, but she was… gone. Erased. She ghosted us, and not knowing where she went was a heavy weight to bear. The uncertainty still eats at Ryan, and it's mind-blowing that I'm here with her and he has no idea. I'm harboring this huge, life-changing secret from him, all because I'm imprisoned and he's back in the city. It's an uncanny and unsettling feeling, especially because my instinct is to go to Ryan with anything new in my life. He won't know for some time.*

Not for the first time, Alex wished they had a pen, a notebook, and Ryan, to accompany their thoughts and loneliness.

CHAPTER 13

I feel alone, left adrift, much like the bloody, burgundy clouds I noted on the day Juneau popped back into my life. Yet unlike those clouds, I'm restricted in movement, circulation severed from my closest family and friends. I'm literally alone here, isolated in my own cell. But I'm neglected in other respects, too: isolated from Ryan, from Jo, and from my family; isolated from my happiness of the summer beaches and the dock and talking honestly with Jo; isolated from Kieran, however conflicted my feelings for them are right now.

As isolated from my classmates as I felt before, now I'm even further removed, physically removed so I don't create "unnecessary distractions" for others. My variance is apparently something to be hidden, feared, to be ashamed of, and to suppress rather than to celebrate. Or so they want me to believe – hell, after everything that's happened, I almost do believe it.

I suspected that there used to be a time and place in which gender variance and a free spectrum of presentations and identities existed. What a utopia! In order for an institution like the Foundation for the Protection of Normative Gender to be created, for small-minded bigots to cement such heinous groundwork, there had to have been some "before time," a time in which variance, or rather, every gender, was accepted and encouraged. Where there are free people and ideologies, there are always equally narrow-minded people seeking to conquer, squash, and rein in those ideologies, to reign over those people and to Other them.

Why am I an Other?

The FPNG and those who support and perpetuate its policies seek to erase me. Worse, they wish to write all Others like me out of existence. My stomach groans and somersaults at the thought. I'm giving myself indigestion.

What is "normative gender," when you break it down? Who defines normative gender? Who says that it consists of merely binaries? Those in power do; white, cisheteronormative men who have no business interfering with the welfare of trans and nonbinary people do. To perpetuate and enforce those binaries means establishing a "normative" society, or so the FPNG says. But why? Is their understanding of their own gender identity so shaky that they must control ours? What is the purpose of endangering our lives and happiness, of infringing on our rights? To refine the visible gender landscape of our world? Why? Is it refining, or are we propelling ourselves backward into some preconceived, primordial state that's been falsely constructed by those with power and influence?

When we deconstruct the pillars, the arguments, and the false fortifications behind those arguments, what's left? The pillars and foundation are hollow, insubstantial, and so are the arbitrary and inflammatory claims from which they were cast. The infrastructure of this system is injected with hot air, and the pathetic part is that most people follow it blindly, accept it as some sort of gospel truth. There is no singular truth.

The multiplicity of truth is a mindfuck, and therefore we, as imperfect humans, tend to construct our own versions of the truth to maintain a tenuous foothold on the slim balance beam on which we tiptoe through our lives.

I'm a sensitive, emotional soul, but there were very few times in my life in which I was physically repulsed by something. However, this is one of those occasions.

I am not legally protected on any governmental level as a nonbinary transgender person. Those rights are reserved for binary individuals, and as evidenced by the FPNG's existence, discrimination against me is even government- and state-mandated. Even if (when?) I escape this accursed prison, I am still adrift, unprotected. Under the law, gender is a binary condition and immutable insofar as cisgender people are concerned. While binary trans people are accepted and mostly safeguarded under these regulations, anti-transgender discriminative mindsets still persist. That's the thing about hate: it's tempting and surprisingly easy to mindlessly consume and disseminate. The law is indelibly linked to federal programs, including education and healthcare, and to the national Department of Health and Human

Services. Gender is an explicit and uniform definition; there's currently zero recognition of gender as a fluid identity.

My rights don't matter one iota to anyone in power, which is why I'm sitting here.

What radical movement do we have to catalyze in order to change these policies?

Is this status quo immutable, or can we rend it in two?

Could a time exist in which Kieran and I, and hell, even Ryan, could truly be ourselves? Be outspoken, recognized, proud, and validated?

I want to be heard and to be taken seriously. I'm torn between harboring a healthy amount of that shame that has been instilled in me, pressed upon me like a heavy thumb into an impressionable piece of clay, and harboring equally conflicting senses of pride and delicious defiance, itching to strike back.

But changing policies wouldn't automatically change people's opinions about nonbinary and gender nonconforming people, would it? Hate is hate. So, what's the point of resistance? Subsistence is so much easier, simpler.

But acceptance, even on a minute scale among friends and closest circles? Man, that is something significant.

Just then, Alex's ears picked up a knock at their cell door, and they fell from their grim contemplation of what could be. Not even bothering to sling their feet across the bed, Alex prepared to greet who they assumed would be Juneau, stopping by with their dinner. They almost called out her name – the J was even on the tip of their tongue – when Officer Paine barged in with his typically stern demeanor. "Dinner time. Eat, inmate." Paine perched Alex's less-than-scrumptious, mealy dinner of mystery meat and smashed peas on their sink and promptly slammed the door behind him.

This close call reminded Alex that here, in the Panoptic, they would be wise not to call Juneau by name until they got out of here. *If* they got out of here. Until they escaped, they'd do well to mind themselves.

Alexandra Cesario is a wholly different person. Oppressed.

The sound of an echoing sob pricked at Alex's ear. Recalling what Juneau said about every two cells sharing an air vent, they located it and plopped down. "Xavier?" they whispered, hesitation cracking their voice to such a degree that they weren't certain he would even hear them.

It was silent for a long while, nothing but the static hum of dead air. The prisoner on the other end of the shaft halted the low sobs in his throat, pitched them back, and attempted to gulp them down as Alex's voice probed into the dark vent once more.

Whispering loudly, "Xavier? Is that you?"

Silence and air.

Next, a grunt, a cough, and a robust clearing of the throat. "Who… who's there? What do you want?" *It is him.* The despair dripped from his every syllable like a wet blanket dragging down an already drenched dog.

"It's me, Alex."

"Alex?" Xavier's tone lifted slightly as he uttered their name, perhaps lightening at the knowledge that a friend was close by.

"Yeah, it's me. Some place, huh?"

"It's definitely not what I pictured. I had a flashy, state-of-the-art prison in mind, not some a rundown, Kilmainham Gaol lookalike. I'm miserable."

"You and me both. I'd wager that the actual Kilmainham is better maintained than this hellhole."

"Alex, how did you know I was next to you?"

"I have a friend who…" Unsure if their conversation would remain entirely undetected, or if their voices would carry and somehow reverberate past the metal air shafts into the Panoptic's atrium where someone might overhear, Alex stopped. "Someone I know told me you were housed next to me, so I took a chance. I, uh, I heard you crying."

"No need to sound embarrassed for me, Alex. I'm not, just self-pitying. This sucks. I'm cold, I'm lonely, and I miss Dakota."

Alex took the chance at Xavier's pause to ask the question nudging at their mind since the airport. "I know we didn't get much of a chance to chat before. So, what's your story? How did you get here?"

"Well, I assumed they had a warrant out for me since that nonbinary meeting. I have no idea if that's true or not, I'm not sure how, or if they identified me. But I was also careless. I see that now.

You know what they say about hindsight, right? I wanted to continue Shay's work of providing a small support group for a few friends I knew. Basically, I revealed too much in an online chat. I wasn't thinking clearly, perhaps from nerves or excitement, and the FPNG pinged the words 'nonbinary' and 'meeting.' A few cronies showed up at my house, confiscated my phone, and here I am. I was only trying to do right by those of us who were left, Alex.

"There was zero chance that I would stand by and let our community, our fellows, rot in loneliness. But, here I am." Xavier's voice faltered as he uttered the word *loneliness*, and an unspoken understanding of the oppression, discrimination, isolation, and erasure that Alex also felt filled the stretch of silence. Alex acknowledged a complete, empathic understanding of not only the internal repressions harbored as a result of being a marginalized individual, but the oppression exacted by their society.

"And you?" Xavier asked.

"Someone turned me in, but I'm not sure who. I don't know if you knew where we were when they stopped the truck, but they seized me at Springfield International Airport. I'd just returned from a trip to see family in the Pacific Northwest over the break with my sister, and three goons came at me. Why are most of the FPNG officers men, anyway?"

"Cishet men like to maintain an old-school, "normalized" status quo. White, cishet men."

"Truer words were never spoken."

"So, what happens now? We rot in here, too?"

Alex couldn't believe their words as they spoke them. They had promised themselves they'd keep their head down, that they'd be careful, but the words came out anyway. "No, we don't. I'm tired of this shit, exhausted from this marginalization, and I know you are, too. We stay put for now, but…"

"But?"

Skating on wafer-thin ice, Alex clapped their hands over their mouth, physically keeping themselves from revealing Juneau's nebulous, theoretical plan of escape, the words, "Juneau and I have a plan," dancing on their tongue. Drawing themselves back from the precipice, Alex said, "But you never know."

"Hmph, our reality is unlikely to change, Alex."

Unless we change it for ourselves, they thought. Alex found themselves processing their circumstances much like the stages of grief as they grieved their loss of freedom: denial, anger, depression, acceptance, and finally, action. Alex characterized their current state as walking the line between anger and acceptance. They were angry as all hell at normative society and the compliant people who actively conspired against their well-being. Anger was fine, but to manifest change, swift and certain action eventually had to be taken. Using that anger to *fuel* action, that was the key. Strong, definitive emotions form the cornerstone of action. After all, wasn't it a similar, definitive, very real hatred and intolerance of nonbinary people that resulted in their arrest in the first place?

Inaction will get us nowhere. Our lives would be a never-ending, torturous stasis.

"You'll see, Xavier. We have to believe in ourselves in some capacity. Right now, that's all we have. I'm not sure how much I believe my own words, but I'm trying my darndest."

A long, drawn echo of a sigh was Xavier's only reply. The two retreated into their respective, private silences, an unspoken agreement that the conversation had ended for now and that further introspection would be their only company for the remainder of the evening.

What day is it now? Alex asked themselves, with the shocking realization that they had no clue. Counting, keeping track, and compartmentalization were Alex's bread and butter, and now they were adrift in a sea of uncertainty with but a few buoys to which they could cling: Juneau and her plan, Xavier's sparse company, the drive that Ryan would most certainly have if he were in this situation, and the belief that freedom was close at hand. *How could Xavier feel so hopeless, given his previous determination to support others like us, to protect his nonbinary siblings? Just like that, no hope? Is he still processing?*

Our survival modes are as individual as we are, I suppose. If I could just write right now. If I could just write...

CHAPTER 14

At dinner the following evening, Juneau asked, "So, can we count on you, Alex?" They had zero clue what day it was, just that every two days they expected a visit from Juneau. Theirs was a two-way hourglass that rocked back and forth like a toddler, ticking in alternate degrees of vastly accelerated days that all blurred together and slow, sluggish sifts akin to wet sand through a plastic beach sieve. Alex could smell the low tide and hear the rush of the morning waves if they closed their eyes hard enough and imagined holding a shell to their ear. That sweet, salty, seaweed smell, the hushing peace and calm of the mild, easterly summer winds, mild for New England, at least, at seventy degrees Fahrenheit. That was paradise. And for a moment, Alex cold-shouldered Juneau's slightly annoyed, furrowed brow and questioning look to soak up the rich, luscious memory.

All Alex recalled about that day was that the sunset had been watermelon-colored; the bright green tint in the sky was a delicious surprise, and a magnificent complement to the fruit-punch pink that bled across the heavens. Little pin pricks of clouds were so dark they assumed the identities of seeds.

Alex escaped to no avail. Juneau's mounting insistence and waving hands across Alex's eyes sucked them back into the brutal present. "Count on me for what?" That sandy, summer wind could have easily carried away the weak hush in their voice.

"To help." At her last word, Juneau's eyes bulged with knowing emphasis in lieu of verbal explanation, lest she risk revealing too much.

"You need me for that? I thought you had it... handled? People assigned, and all that. Like you said – ready for action."

Alex's lack of conviction, for which they had only yesterday mentally berated Xavier, tripped up not only Juneau but themselves momentarily, and they felt themselves slipping backward, reverting to their safe, sheltered mindset. *No, I can't rest on my laurels*, Alex thought. They wanted action; they felt conviction as real as the fire in their belly and a burning determination to work their way back to Ryan and Jo. *I'm scared of the repercussions if we are caught. The best laid plans are thwarted if the enemy has more resources, more bodies, and fears losing power and control.* Alex admitted as much to Juneau, who nodded in understanding.

"Sure, Alex, but we need more people. To fly under the radar, we only have about half a dozen of us stationed in the intimate fleet of guards here. I'm sure you can understand that not everyone jumps at the opportunity to work directly in the lion's den, in a prison on the remote summit of a mountain plopped between three warring weather patterns almost seven thousand feet above sea level. Think about it: if too many of us volunteered in the same lot, there'd be even more probing questions, too much suspicion. In the Panoptica, questions are the enemy."

"Gods forbid we ever question the system," Alex replied sarcastically.

Juneau plowed on past the cynicism and said, stern and serious, "Yes, exactly."

"So, what's your weapon? The fulcrum with which you intend to pry open the Panoptic's rusting doors?"

"You are."

"Me? Don't kid yourself, Juneau. I'm not some holier-than-thou chosen one. I'm just like the rest of us. I'm just Alex."

Juneau sighed and offered a gentle smile. "Yes, it may appear that way. There are no 'chosen ones' among us, but there are people with conviction. Conviction is power. It's not that we're chosen by some ordained, omnipotent power; we *choose* to take action. The plural you, all the nonbinary and nonbinary trans folks and gender variant folks locked in here merely for having the courage to exist and live by their own truths, that's our weapon. You. All of you."

Alex crossed their arms, unsure of how Juneau and company (and Alex, apparently) were going to enact this rebel plan. It seemed too entrenched in theoretic imagination. Sure, the plan may have been plotted with the utmost care, but it was tinted with an aura of nascent idealism that Alex wasn't sure was solid enough to carry it through to fruition, or to inspire others to fight on their behalf. The nonbinary folk in the Northeast Panoptic, including those posing as guards, outweighed the oppressors in sheer numbers, Alex held little doubt about that. But instilling faith and confidence in the imprisoned, no matter how determined they were to get home, was another matter altogether.

"So?" Juneau's eyes bored into Alex, praying her stare would elicit the answer she wanted.

It may as well be me. Who else will be brave enough to step forward? "You got me. I'm in."

An animated, full-bodied jump for joy and a hug probably weren't approved in guard-to-prisoner contact protocol, so Juneau settled for a wide smile and a low fist pump.

"Hell yes! All right. Awesome." She composed herself just in time for…

Knock knock.

"Shit." Juneau performed a quick about-face and threw open Alex's cell door. Officer Paine stood in its frame, the dizzying shine of the Panoptic guard tower's mirrors making Alex's head spin with a kaleidoscope of reflections; they even saw an imitation of their small form in those mirrors, too. Following protocol, Juneau saluted Paine and stood aside to allow him into the cell.

"Anderson, what in God's name are you doing in here with the door closed?" he pried. Alex dare not flinch or gulp, fearing they would betray guilt, and from there, suspicion and distrust.

"Sir," Juneau replied rapidly and with confidence, "I was prepping Miss Cesario for her first scheduled reform class tomorrow. What she should expect, proper behavior, and the usual threats." Alex wondered, *What are the usual threats? What reform classes?*

"Hmph. Even still. Given your previously flawless record, I would think you'd know better than to close the door to an inmate's cell without proper backup. Especially," and his eyes darted like sharp arrows at Alex, "a repeat offender such as this one."

What the hell does he mean by that? So, they were *watching me! And Ryan thought I was paranoid.*

"I'm sorry, sir." Juneau's answers betrayed not a hint of dishonesty. If Alex didn't know her, she would presume Juneau meant every word. "I'll rectify my mistake at once."

"See that you do." Officer Paine gestured for Juneau to follow him out and she did without a look back, slamming the solid cell door behind her.

***

They resisted the urge to dwell on the subject of "reform classes" and what torture awaited them, but Alex needed not wait long to discover what Juneau had meant. As widely circulated as the literature was, FPNG propaganda merely promised "immediate removal from the city and mandated rehabilitation." The Foundation was ominously vague about what they meant by "rehabilitation." Alex was struck by how little they knew about what was coming next, what prolonged imprisonment by the gender police looked like. Since their arrest in Springfield, they didn't have a dang clue what would happen to them, what activities and programs they'd have to endure. Alex thrived on routine and structure, and this entire experience was the very antithesis of that norm. They felt swept along in an endless current, the next twist or turn as unpredictable as the one before. Things in the Northeast Panoptic felt maddeningly and surprisingly unscripted and played by ear, like a crumb one brushes away to vacuum up at a later date. Was this purposeful disorientation, or evidence of carelessness?

For the rigid binary gender and presentation standards the FPNG enforced, their time in the Panoptic so far had been decidedly unstructured, save for mealtimes twice a day.

Until the next morning.

About an hour after breakfast, all the nonbinary kids, teens, and folks from the train were released from their cells and shepherded into a dingy, first-floor classroom that featured a whiteboard and several anatomical sketches. Alex recognized a few faces here and there, including Xavier. Guards lined the room's entire periphery, standing menacingly still. They nearly jumped when they noticed Juneau among them, but they were forcibly plopped down into a desk at the very front of the room, far away from her. They knew they were in for some biological essentialism bullshit when they noticed two thick posters bolted to the whiteboard: one of a person with a penis, the other of a person with a vagina. Above the bodies, a tidy serif font classified these illustrations as a "man" and a "woman." Alex rolled their eyes, a reflex when confronted with blatant binary bullshit and propaganda.

A Foundation crony in a lab coat slinked into the Reeducation Classroom, but Alex ignored the nametag on his lapel. *Why did it matter who he was?* Alex's eyes refocused, and he dove into his lecture with stilted, rehearsed sentences. "Welcome, ladies and gentlemen, to the Northeast Panoptic. You know why you're here. Your actions brought you here, your choices and your deviant impulses. For reasons understood and communicated between yourselves and those at the Foundation handling your cases, you're here because of your failure to comply with the genders and presentations set forth by law, and thus, you have violated that law by presenting or identifying with a gender or genders strictly prohibited."

The nauseating lecture that followed was a veritable word-for-word rundown of the FPNG's sites, flyers, commercials, and propaganda posters, from "technical" gender terminology, approved presentation guidelines, prohibited presentation factors, biological sexes, required hormonal makeups, and genitals – the works. As he recited the policies and requirements by rote, he had a small ruler that he whacked against the diagrams in front of Alex, and they jumped every time, despite anticipating each blow. Every *thwack* was as much an assault on the two diagrammed humans as on Alex, tangibly stacking up the gender restrictions against them as he enumerated the list.

"Now, you'd *think* these preservative rules would be old news to you. But the Foundation for the Protection of Normative Gender is also rolling out new policies." More slapping of the whiteboard to emphasize his points. "Trans women are already required to undergo bottom surgery as part of their transition. Soon, we will require the same gender confirmation surgery of trans men."

Someone from the back raised their hand and interrupted the speaker. "But sir, and this is an honest question, how will they afford it? Phalloplasty is prohibitively expensive and time-consuming, much as bottom surgery is for trans women."

Whether this person was asking for themselves or another, they were right. *What will Ryan think of this? He has expressed little interest in pursuing this kind of surgery. Will folks who've already legally transitioned be grandfathered in or granted a pass on this requirement?*

Pointing to acknowledge that person in the back, the instructor replied, "Yes, that certainly is a concern. Excellent question. There will be no exceptions granted. Trans men *will* undergo phalloplasty. However, payment plans will be available for those who cannot afford the surgery cost up front. Repayment rates will be determined by income, much like an auto or student loan."

"That could take a long time." The person's voice from the back faded into the quiet crowd of inmates gathered in the classroom.

The lab coat interjected, "Any questions pertaining to your particular case will be addressed at length in your therapy sessions. Please hold all questions until the end of the session." He held up his hand to silence any other outbursts, and then went on. "Now, let's pivot to another matter. The most common and persistent problem among your group in particular is pronoun usage, *incorrect* pronoun usage."

Alex dreaded any talk centered on pronouns. Pronouns were so finicky, so revealing, and therefore, all the more important. Using the "right" pronouns granted access to acceptance, just as the "wrong" resulted in dissent and disapproval.

"Many of you are in severe violation of repeated incorrect pronoun usage. It's vital to remember the two approved sets of pronouns and why we use them: he/him and she/her, both of which correspond with an approved gender.

"This is all 101-level stuff, but it bears repeating since your conduct demonstrates a complete lack of understanding and compliance with these fundamentals.

"Moreover, some of you," and he glared pointedly at a few folks around the room, mentally singling them out amongst their peers, "have felt it necessary to invent your own pronouns. This is deviant. Without the standards set by the Foundation, how are we to gauge the gender of others? Fabricating new pronouns is illegal, and moreover, it creates considerable confusion. Without the kinds of common denominators that pronouns establish, it can be nearly impossible to understand and connect with one another. A shocking number of people are guilty of this deviant crime."

I wonder why this assumption exists, why they've fabricated this disconnect between people with "normative," approved pronouns and those without, Alex thought bitterly. Every word uttered against Alex's community disgusted them. They were just waiting for the man to raise the apparent "issues" with *they* pronouns, and he did not disappoint.

"To that end, I must remind you that using *they* or *them* as pronouns referring to a single person or yourself is demonstrably incorrect, inappropriate, and strictly forbidden by all FPNG measures. As far as traditional semantics and grammar rules direct us, using the first person *they* is grammatically incorrect. The word *they* refers to a plural group, to multiple people. Not one person."

I can't tell if this guy is just ignorant, brainwashed, or a gaslighting liar. Probably all three. Does he not understand that language evolves? I can't believe I'm being subjected to this. It's shocking and disgusting. Why in the hell do they care so much about interfering in other people's lives? What purpose does it serve to control everything? Are they paranoid? Hate, ignorance, and paranoia grease the wheels of this system, I'm sure of it.

Alex wanted to pipe up, no, to scream. To scream and yell and rail against every point Mr. Lab Coat just made and would continue to make over the course of this torturous class. They wanted to critically and categorically deconstruct the very foundation on which the FPNG built these false claims. Every point of their rebuttal laid on the very edge of Alex's tongue, so they shut their mouth all the more firmly, afraid that if they even opened their mouth to sigh or breathe, they'd spew out their "illegal rhetoric."

But someone did have the gall to speak out.

"Sir?"

Is that Xavier's voice? No way, it couldn't be. He was so broken yesterday. He wouldn't dare.

"Yes?"

"Exactly how long will we be here?"

Alex chanced to turn around in their seat just as Xavier finished his question. *What the hell is he doing?*

"What's your name?"

"Xavier, sir."

"Is that your birth name or your chosen name?"

It grosses me out that Lab Coat can even ask that.

"Umm..."

Lab Coat didn't give Xavier the chance to answer. "I don't recall seeing the name 'Xavier' on any of the intake forms I received upon your train's arrival, which leads me to believe that's not your real name. I will answer your question nonetheless. The length of time you remain in the Panoptic depends entirely on your willingness to not only cooperate, but to entrench yourself in the reeducation program and dedicate yourself to reformation and true change. Those factors alone will determine your fate here. Your path is in your hands. But should one continue to resist, well, that's another matter entirely."

In response to that vague yet menacing threat, Xavier retreated as far back into his seat as he could manage. Alex felt similarly and desired nothing more than to shrink into themselves, to disappear. But in this classroom, guards at every elbow, Alex was very visible and felt more exposed than ever, caught in the act of defiance and publicly put on display for FPNG to mock and ridicule.

"Any other questions?" No one moved a muscle. "Any further clarification needed?"

For how quiet the room was, a cough would have echoed as loudly as a roar.

"No? Good. The guards will see you back to your cells. Within the next few days, you will be informed of the date of your first therapy session. Until then, please see that you begin to reorganize your thoughts and outlook. I've ensured each of you will have access to the requisite Bible and a copy of the revised FPNG handbook, the new edition freshly minted this month." Alex didn't remember seeing either of those items in their small cell, but they'd surely be waiting on their bed upon their return.

A dual-headed poisonous viper, as far as I'm concerned. Two forms of propaganda, one purpose unites them.

***

Left without a pen with which they could either write over or scribble out the entirety of the FPNG handbook, they removed it from their bed and placed it on the top of their stainless-steel toilet seat. *It's shit, anyway.* The alarmingly lengthy tome – Alex concluded it had to be at least 300 pages – was bound in black leather with gold, embossed script dancing across the front cover and spine. *Foundation for the Protection of Normative Gender Regulations and Guidelines: A Comprehensive Volume.*

They'd relish the opportunity to rip those pages to shreds, but they suspected that would only invite further punishment and perhaps additional fines for "defacing Foundation property." Instead, Alex found themselves writing creative lines in their head, attempting to come up with as many messages with the letters F, P, N, and G as they could manage.

> **Fear** of **People Not** like the **General** *populace*
> **Fear, Persecution**: **Normative Gesticulations**
> **Fight** *for* **Policies** *purporting* **Normative Gender**
> **Fight** *against* **Policies** *establishing* **Normative Gender**
> **Fake, Palpable, Needless Gentrification**
> **False Promises Need Guarding**
> **Fierce Person**, *but* **Not** a **Girl**

Alex wondered when they'd be allowed to hold a pen and write again. The last piece they'd composed was their poem "FtM," weeks after escaping the clutches of the FPNG, and the night before they'd inadvertently sabotaged themselves at school. The poem itself was inspired, Alex thought; it was the most meaningful piece they'd ever written, and yet it served as a liminal marker of validation between two crappy and life-changing events. Every word matters.

The past few months struck Alex as simultaneously validating and ruthlessly destructive. *Is that how life will always be,* they wondered, *contending with the exponentially rippling repercussions that threaten to consume me as a result of my decisions and the actions of others?* These outside influences both penetrated and reflected off of Alex, opening up new paths of opportunity and forever closing others. With the actions of others just as influential as their own, Alex felt like a medium, a prism, and in another sense, a specter, someone whose own actions made only a nominal impact on their desired outcomes. They'd ended up here, after all. The surreality of the situation overwhelmed them, as it did whenever they stopped to take stock of their surroundings, the full gravity of living that it signified. All that protection, guarded by their parents, by Ryan, by their own sense of self-preservation, it was all for naught now. How silly and ridiculous their worrying seemed in retrospect, if this, the Panoptic, was always the inevitable outcome of their adolescence.

Alex blew out a rough sigh, the kind where you feel your determination and sanity leave your body along with your life force. *What now?*

In fighting, choose with sense and honor. Alex recalled one of the codes from Juneau's official Tang Soo Do manual, the phrase Alex tested her on time and time again before Juneau's intermediary belt tests. It felt like a lifetime ago that Juneau had time for karate and friends. *I'd say this is a pretty reasonable situation in which fighting would be permissible.*

Honor friendship – another one of the Tang Soo Do codes that the federation had instilled in Juneau, and maybe in Alex by extension. Friendship was one of the single greatest bonds between people. Alex would always honor their friendships with Ryan, Juneau, Xavier, and even Kieran, if they were even still friends with them. Alex reminded themselves that Juneau would honor them by fighting to get Alex and the others out of the Panoptic. In order to bring that plan to life, Alex had to participate.

Two days later, Juneau cycled back into Alex's life, the one guiding light as they waited for whatever the Foundation's guards had planned for them next. Alex still didn't know when they'd be meeting with their therapist or what classes they'd be expected to take. There was no time to ask; Juneau made it clear that she had to talk fast.

"Why?" Alex queried.

"Do you want to know the escape plan or not?" she whispered, an impish grin creeping across her face.

CHAPTER 15

In meager morsels over the course of the next week, Juneau unveiled her game plan. Due to Paine's previous interference, Juneau understandably didn't want to risk further infractions; they stood on the edge of the precipice, the tipping point, arms outstretched and ready for the inevitable plunge into the deep, icy waters of the unknown. When Juneau finished laying out her great conspiracy plan, Alex realized they'd have just one week to prep, and they'd all have to act as if nothing was afoot.

"When your train arrived, the Northeast Panoptic almost reached max capacity. Two weeks from now, another train is rolling in, not too many prisoners this time, but extra hands, nonetheless. The difference is that many of these folks got themselves arrested for this very purpose. Many others who are here now did the same. They all know what's at stake."

"What's their purpose?"

"Distraction. Our folks outside will cause a ruckus, drawing guards out like antibodies. In that moment, we strike."

"How exactly will we do that? What kind of a ruckus? Do we know for sure it'll work?"

"We're still hammering out the details, but no, we're not sure."

As Juneau sketched the plan with her words, she seemed to think it was as straightforward as it could get. Alex wasn't so sure. They perceived several loose ends, weaknesses that hinged on many pieces going exactly right, and Alex believed that the most active ingredient in this concoction was sheer, dumb luck.

Juneau was still talking. "I've been working to maintain a spotless reputation for a reason. The elder, more senior-ranking guards always accompany us newbies on our shifts. Until now. A select few of us have earned our way out of that mentorship program, and we've pulled some strings to make sure that we're scheduled on the same, midday Saturday shift. Since the guards like to take it easy on Saturdays, it's the most undesirable shift of the week, which works in our favor. Every single cell can be unlocked individually with our IDs, for those who have the proper clearance." Juneau winked. "As of today, yours truly has top-tier clearance. Just in time, eh? Thankfully, that misstep with Paine was excused. Blessed be."

"I'll say," Alex agreed.

"We recognize that we'll still have a headcount disadvantage at that point. So, we're unlocking a chosen few of you from your cells to bolster our plan, people who we know won't flake under pressure, who have taken similar risks before. You're among that group, Alex."

"What's my part to play in this big, moving puzzle?"

"I'll get to that."

***

On Wednesday, Juneau continued. "We'll wait for the train to arrive from Springfield. It's critical that the other FPNG officers are spread as thinly as possible when the iron strikes. Some will be stationed outside to greet the train, some will be in the intake rooms, and some will be unloading the train. Aside from those remaining in the watchtower, very few boots will be on the ground in the atrium and actual main prison area."

"What about the risk of being seen? Are there cameras in the nooks and crannies of this place? What will I be helping with?"

"Patience, I'm getting to that. But you guessed wrong, Alex. Do you know how old this place is?" Alex shook their head. "Well, neither do I, I admit. It's old enough for me to know that they'd have to rip into these walls in order to rewire and install a state-of-the-art prison video monitoring system. It's all people power here. There *are* guards in the watchtower, though. That's a critical feature of this place; the 360-degree tower is designed to do what cameras would in their stead: to monitor each cell in full view.

"Inside that tower is another key piece of our plan: the universal cell switchboard. The one innovation this junked up place does have is an automatic door release for each cell. The catch is that the cells cannot be opened all at once, just one by one. That's an obvious safety precaution."

Alex noted, "Unless there's a fire or something."

"Woah, that's very true. What a grim point, Alex. Not sure why I had never thought of that before. Knowing these guards like I do, if that were to happen or some insane storm blew in and we had to abort mission, most of these guys would jump ship and save themselves as quickly as possible."

"That's promising. Are we not real people to the Foundation? Are we subhuman? Truly, Juneau, what do you think?"

Juneau's downcast eyes gave Alex the answer they sought. "Don't make me say it, I think you already know."

***

They met again on Friday. "The flurry of activity will be difficult to coordinate, but it's our best shot. One of us guards will go distract whoever is commanding the watchtower, and therefore the switchboard, and they'll strategically release a few inmates, including you and Xavier."

"Thank the gods."

"This next bit requires the utmost stealth. I'll sneak y'all off to the prison bathrooms."

"Which one?"

"Whichever is unoccupied. I'll have spare, freshly laundered uniforms waiting. You'll both change into them. We just need enough cover to get back to the tower."

"And there we will help whoever is stationed there with the distracted guard?"

"Exactly."

***

On Sunday, just six days before the next train's fated arrival at the Northeast Panoptic, Juneau shared the rest of her action plan.

"Here's the final stage of the coup: We scale the watchtower using the emergency staircases on either side, restrain the guard at the top, and start releasing everyone, cell by cell. If we're lucky, we may have another group rendezvous with us there to assist."

"Easy peasy," Alex remarked with thick sarcasm. "What then, Juneau?"

"We fight like hell and get the fuck out of this place."

"And after we dismantle this hellish Panoptic?"

"Haha, let's see how far we get first," Juneau laughed.

"So, what's my role, specifically?"

"I just told you…"

"Yes, yes, I know. But what qualifies me to help with this part of the plan? Couldn't anyone do this, reinforce your efforts to conquer the watchtower? Why did you want me among that group instead of someone else? I don't have any experience in combat or subterfuge."

"Honestly, Alex? It's because I trust you. I trust in your ability to stick by my side, and I trust you not to run if things get dicey."

Seems legit enough of a reason for me. "Anyway, I thought you said this plan was bulletproof?"

"Oh Alex, it's far from it. I'm not so naïve to assume that any of this will be seamless or simple, but it's our best chance to destroy this station for good. Yes, shit could go down. But that's the risk we assume, right?"

"What about the others?"

"The others of us?" Alex shook their head deeply at Juneau's response. Juneau may be leading this revolt, but Alex wondered if she really, fully understood the macrocosmic scope of the societal reality.

"The other Panoptica. Haven't you given any thought to the wider issue here?"

Juneau scratched at her chin. Alex detected the barest hint of five o'clock shadow. "I hate to admit this, but to be frank, we had not. I'm narrowly focused on this one task, this one Panoptic. When we are free, we can talk about the future."

"For real?" Alex was astonished, actually flabbergasted at the lack of foresight. Since Alex met her, Juneau had an obsessive tendency to think through every minute detail, play out every aspect of each possibility of every scenario, and then analyze them for the best results. In this case, she'd been so focused that it seemed she forgot to remove her blinders. "We both know this is doable, even if it is a long shot. But dismantling one prison won't crumble the foundation of, well, the Foundation, or the whole system. At best, the Foundation will be temporarily weakened when we crumble one of their main pillars. How will that help us overall?"

"Alex, rein yourself in here. I haven't thought that far ahead because this *is* a long shot. You just said it yourself. I'm not going to promise certain outcomes without knowing for sure I can deliver on this first step."

"Again, I repeat: how will this help those of us who are disadvantaged? We'll run out of the frying pan and into the fire. Nothing has changed in Springfield." Alex could tell Juneau was starting to steam at the perceived incredulity of their words. A small vein throbbed on her temple. Why should they argue when one of their best friends delivered an escape plan to them on a silver platter? Moreover, their time together today was waning, the sand in the hourglass spilling over with every wasted word, every wasted second.

Nonetheless, Juneau maintained her composure. "Well, first of all, it'll help our immediate situation: it'll help *you* get out of this shit hole. Second, it will expose the weaknesses in the FPNG system, both to themselves and to the public; I'm sure some reporter will catch hold of a juicy cover story in which nonbinary and gender nonconforming folks got into this prison undetected and infiltrated the administration. It will show that the Foundation's core force is spread too thin, and that leaving one of these prisons *is* possible without "reeducation." And most importantly, our actions will show the world that nonbinary and GNC folks still possess the power, determination, and courage to fight back against the forces that wish to quell us."

Before Alex could open their mouth, Juneau closed the conversation. "Gotta go," she said, and left them behind with nothing but a twinge of shame and their now-cold minced meat and pea dinner.

***

Bedtime for the inmates drew the day's light from their cells and back into the expanse of the rotunda atrium, and the evening spotlights of the central watchtower lit up in response. A small night-light in the upper corner of Alex's cell cast a dull, ambient glow, just enough for them to find their way to the toilet in the middle of the night, and to make their body visible to the guards completing their nightly rounds.

What bedtime didn't draw from Alex was their voice, and they found themselves yet again whispering across the vented airspace to Xavier in hushed, sleep-laden words.

"What are you going to do when we get out of here?" Xavier sent the question off to Alex's ear, each laying stomach-down on their cots, hanging over their own vent. Alex answered only in the theoretical, unsure if Juneau had filled Xavier in on the plan.

"Oh man, solid question." It *was* a good question, and Alex didn't have a good answer. Their first inclination was to say that they'd love to move away from the city after graduation, maybe to northern Maine where they could see more of Kieran and apply to a few colleges, but then it struck Alex, mid-sentence: "Will I be able to graduate on time? If I miss too much school while detained here? Hell, I'll be an FPNG fugitive; maybe I won't be able to go back at all."

"No idea, Alex. I actually hadn't thought about that, about the long-term. I'm pretty much just focused on survival at this point."

"I don't know what I want out of life or what to do," Alex said. "That's a pretty strange position for me. I always think about the next thing, the next opportunity, book, path, goal, plan. Maybe it's the city dweller in me, but I'm always go, go, go, what's next? What else do I need to do? What project can I complete? My eyes are always on the future."

"Then you forget about the present," Xavier offered softly.

"You're right. So, theoretically, what will you do when you get out?"

Alex imagined Xavier was shrugging. "I dunno. Go back home and find Dakota. I miss zir and want to start things again. Honestly, I crave spending time with ze, my other partner, and my family. I have simple desires, really."

"That sounds wonderful."

Alex heard shuffling from Xavier's end of the vent and the conversation faded. *Perhaps he's off to bed. I loathe not knowing what's to come. Chaos abounds in uncertainty.*

What do I want to do with my life? Truthfully, I want more than anything to escape Springfield, regardless of how my parents or

Jo feel about it. I want to graduate and escape the public eye, which could be possible if our escape plan is successful.

I see two outcomes here. Scenario One: If we fail, we'll be thrown back into these cells, subjected to some new form of cruelty or punishment that extends beyond the "reeducation" classroom. Who the hell knows what would be in store for us? If I'm ever released from here, which is doubtful after a jailbreak attempt, you bet your butt the Foundation will monitor me closely, and the same goes for Juneau, Xavier, Shay, and all the others. Geez, from school, the nonbinary group and crouching in that restaurant during the nor'easter, to the summer chilling with Jo, mum, and dad at the vacation house, to Kieran – lifetimes have passed.

Scenario Two: We fight, we escape, we flee from this wretched place, and my life is in my own hands again. Maybe my future will be completely up to me to determine. We will be free. Happy, hopefully. But to get there, we'll have to fight for it.

This potential euphoria is sitting just beyond of the tips of my fingers: the euphoria of maybe seeing Kieran again, of hugging Ryan – I miss that goof way too much – of seeing him reunite with Juneau, of being myself, of writing, of sleeping in my own bed.

When, not if, I survive this, I'm dedicating a significant portion of my time to writing. I want the pen in my hand or the keys beneath my fingers, any medium so long as I can write again. To have those tools taken away, to be robbed of even the simplest pen and paper, it's debilitating. I feel constricted and asphyxiated, like I'm searching for peaceful sleep in an uncomfortable huddle with restless limbs and no room to stretch. My hands are twitching.

I'm itching for self-expression.

Finally feeling gender euphoria again would be life changing. True gender euphoria, and to be validated by your friends, your peers, and your appearance is the touchstone of happiness. To wear whatever I want whenever I want, to have variance and fluidity in my expression, and to not be judged, or at least not actively and legally persecuted. That smells like freedom. To be respected, protected, proud, and accepted, and to not be afraid to step out and not only express myself, but say how I feel and stand up for others. That rings

141

of utopia. In this envisioned life, I imagine sporting a bold shirt with the word Genderfluid plastered across the chest for all to read, and not being arrested on sight. To chop off my hair, to adorn stereotypically men's clothing, and to identify outside of my assigned birth gender, should I choose. I'd even go by "Alex" and use they/them pronouns as people get warmed up. That's the dream: a world with accepted fluid gender and gender expression. Is this outcome achievable? Feasible? Laughable?

I don't even know what prolonged gender euphoria is supposed to feel like. I've merely tasted snippets, little nibbles of what could be. To feel that all the time, I'd likely cry with how overwhelmed I would feel, break down with the glory of it all.

Gender euphoria is the higher power to which I endlessly pray.

Alex looked to the heavens, which for them was the bland, gray cell ceiling, as if mimicking prayer, but they knew they wouldn't pray, not really. All these years later, the Our Fathers, Hail Marys, and Act of Contritions were still bolted to the sides of their brain from their Catholic upbringing and catechism education. Remembering the words was mere muscle memory, and they said them that night with ease, though not directing their intention to any higher power in particular. On their fifth recitation of the Hail Mary, Alex's eyes slowly slipped shut. Drawing the light from their surroundings and into the corners of their eyes put into stark contrast, like a laser focus, the snow globe of a storm that wound itself in circles outside their window: one flake trying to catch its own tail, then the tail of another. Whipping in wisps around and around, the scene looked so perfect to Alex, from their limited view of it, that it seemed unreal. Not that it was too early in the year for snow, but it was remarkable for the storm to come on so quickly and to so closely resemble the perfect, uniform flakes of a snow globe bought at any tourist shop in a seaside town, maybe with a lighthouse in the middle and a gull or two racing across the sky.

CHAPTER 16

James Bay serenaded Alex as they clutched Kieran's hand and drew them into the crowd of other queer humans waiting, anticipating their entrance on the Maine Street Club's dance floor. Rainbow uplights and spotlights directed their brilliance onto the central disco ball, which hung like a retro chandelier in the center of the dance floor, clouding their vision just as much as the two drinks each had downed at the bar half an hour ago. Kieran swam through the swarm of people flocking behind them to the floor, some already jumping up onto the stage and swinging lasciviously around the stripper poles bolted there.

Kieran sang to themselves, mouthing James Bay's lilting lyrics as they swayed in motion with the music.

Alex sang in response, an octave lower than their October voice, when Kieran had seen them last. Alex had been on testosterone for their Hormone Replacement Therapy for six months to the day. Today was a celebration of them.

Of us.

Kieran wore the very same outfit from their coffee date with Alex that first day in Springfield. They loved being open about their fluidity and encouraging Alex to do the same. Or maybe it was the other way around – maybe Alex was encouraging *them*. Kieran loved seeing Alex happy, finally unashamed, in a world that wouldn't disgrace them like their old one had.

Kieran loved Alex.

"I'll tell Alex tonight, I swear," Kieran mumbled to themselves, certain that the thrumming, deafening beat from the DJ's speakers would suck the sound from their words. But seeing their lips move, Alex kissed Kieran and said, "What?"

"Nothing," Kieran mouthed, their nerves silencing and paralyzing them. They grabbed Alex's hips as an anchor, steadying their vision, which got increasingly blurry the more their drinks hit them. *I've never felt more alive than this moment*, they thought.

James Bay reminded Kieran to be reckless, to stay caught up in the moment, to not waver or overthink. *I want to be hopeful, too. Is hope no longer unattainable? Who granted me the freedom and permission to be happy in this utopia? To finally thrive? Is this how people feel when they're high? Or in love? Or both?*

I don't want to change myself, or alter myself to conform to others' expectation of some unrealized ideal. More than life itself, I desire for the system to bend to me, to evolve to accommodate whoever I want to be. Anything less is an alteration. Alex says I am just as valid however I dress, however I look. Imagine finding someone like that.

I want to marry this person someday, Kieran admitted to themselves, wondering if the thought was wild. Was it reckless or daring?

Alex's eyes swiveled with drunk abandon, refocusing on Kieran after each trip their eyes made around the room. *Sometimes, you keep looking and looking but the obvious answer is right under your nose, leaning in to kiss you at that very moment*, Alex thought, welcoming the embrace from their partner.

Alex and Kieran locked themselves together, intertwined irrevocably on that dance floor, the melody, the other people, the light splashing them from the disco ball above and then bleeding away. All else was numb but the pair's focus on one another.

However, just then, sudden sunshine pried the bottom of Alex's eyelids open, and they almost fainted at the sight of Kieran, whose body was entirely translucent white, a specter of the fully formed partner swaying with them only a moment before, who had been aglow with rainbow disco spots. The only spots Alex saw now were those across their vision, cast from the treacherous sunlight above and behind them somewhere. Did they dance for so long that the sun came up?

Alex twisted around to locate its source. *Who turned the sun on?* They blinked to clear their fuzzy mind and their eyes of those relentless sunspots, and as they did, their prison cell window faded into view, and Alex's throat constricted in a bitter choking cry as they realized the club had been but the shadow of a dream and they were now awake. Awake and still imprisoned.

These realizations bubbled to the surface of Alex's mind, as did Prospero's very last spoken lines from *The Tempest*, another of their Shakespearean favorites second only to *Twelfth Night*. They cried harder as they recalled them:

> *As you from crimes would pardon'd be,*
> *Let your indulgence set me free.*

***

An hour later, Alex pried their eyes open, crusted shut from crying. All at once, the gravity of the day hit them: Alex didn't know how many days they'd been imprisoned in the Panoptic, but today was day zero, breakout day. Unprepared to start the day, clinging to the lush happiness their dream had instilled in them, Alex refused to sit up just yet, refused to prepare, to have the day hail them in and require the serious concentration and effort that would follow. Alex was frozen in their own indecision: should they force themselves awake and begin to mentally steady themselves for the arduous day ahead, or should they indulge themselves in the latent memory of their dream once more?

In lieu of rising, Alex tipped their head back as far as it would go and aimed their gaze at their barred window, a symbol of their freedom – so close and yet just out of reach. In actuality, the sun wasn't as bright as they'd first thought in that surrealist club, but the pale light, the color of a freshly born chick, nonetheless seeped its way into the cell and across Alex's eyes.

Beyond the glow, Alex detected the milky remains of a fuchsia sunrise, speckled with splotches of dusty red. The sky was pure beauty, with the faintest dust of cloud cover. *Strange that the snowstorm blew over so fast.* But the temporarily peaceful sky foretold nothing for the remainder of the day. The weather on Mount Washington was more unpredictable than any summit on the eastern seaboard.

Red sky at night, sailors' delight. Red sky in morning, sailors take warning.

As the sun rose further into the sky, Alex marveled at the diffraction of the red rays around the morning's altocumulus clouds.

They repeated the sailors' token phrase of good and bad fortune maybe twenty times before finally flinging their feet over the side of their cot, standing up, stretching down to their toes and slowly rolling themselves up, vertebra by vertebra. They peed, dressed in their all-black uniform, and waited for their breakfast.

As far as Alex knew, the key players were in place. What worried them the most were the other players, the cogs, the plots that Alex didn't yet know, of which they were not privy. Were the oils of their mechanism properly greased? All theoretical situations drawn out and tested? When Juneau had pieced together the plan for Alex, she'd inspired them. The way Juneau spoke, success seemed definite, or at least a likely probability. Now, in this critical moment with the weight of the day, of their past, and of the tasks still yet to be accomplished blanketing them in uncertainty, Alex felt like the smallest ladybug next to the Matterhorn of the Swiss Alps. What impact could their tiny measures have against a mountain? To overthrow the Northeast Panoptic felt impossible enough, never mind contending with the FPNG after that, or the possibility of dismantling other Panoptica. In the harsh light of the day, it seemed like a child's dream.

They stared at their hydrated oatmeal after the punctual breakfast delivery and weighed these heavy thoughts, running the risk of scaring themselves into inaction. Were they really about to untie all of Juneau and Xavier and Shay's good work and intentions with their private, practical, poisonous thoughts? It seemed that way, until Alex considered the consequence of inaction, of doing absolutely nothing.

For one, being forced to live the remainder of their days marked as a "woman," as "female," as this one specific gender in accordance with FPNG guidelines was the worst potential outcome Alex faced. And yet, that very outcome was assured if they did not follow through with their promise to assist Juneau and the others.

Juneau is relying on me, remember? She specifically sought me out because of my lifelong trustworthiness and commitment to fulfill my promises. Who else but me could fill that role?

Channeling their raw disgust for that version of a lifelong dysphoria stirred action in them and reignited their conviction. Never mind thinking about their friends, their allies, the rest of the people trapped in the Northeast Panoptic, with their own lives and paths and stories of love and loss and longing. If these other folks didn't possess that same anger and conviction, if they weren't willing to fight for and advocate for themselves, should Alex? If they didn't, who would fight on their behalf?

No one, was the cruel, brutal answer Alex could not ignore. They also pondered the repercussions of inaction upon their arrival back in Springfield. What would Ryan say when Alex told him, *if* Alex could bear the words, that they'd idly sat by as Juneau and others risked their lives for the sake of their whole community? If Alex didn't participate, they would be all the more embarrassed if Juneau succeeded, slim chance as there was. Disappointed wouldn't begin to describe how Alex would feel in that instance. Not only disappointed but shamed. Shame, disgust, disappointment: these were three emotions with which Alex was well acquainted, but they couldn't bear the thought of attaching such weighty feelings to one moment of cowardice.

After hashing their thoughts out, Alex knew they'd be joining Juneau. After all, Alex was sure that one of the Foundation's main goals was to overwhelm those who would resist with the immensity of the FPNG's resources. The Foundation still had power, but Alex now knew that the omnipotent control they thought the Foundation possessed just months ago was but a foggy façade. Alex forced the sloppy, now-cold oats down their throat, justifying eating as their stomach turned over like a clothes dryer with the reality that they didn't know when their next meal would be, and they very much needed to fortify their body with some energy for the afternoon.

Alex feebly attempted to pass the remainder of that morning by meditating, with varying degrees of focus, but they could not attain peace or mindfulness. Their perception of time was like a cruel VCR player, skipping forward, backward, and halting in place as some omnipresent power punched the play, fast-forward, and pause buttons in random succession in a dizzying punishment. One minute, they sought to cherish every moment of silence and relative peace they could before the onslaught of relentless, chaotic entropy to come; in another minute, during various periods of pauses and slow plays, Alex wanted more than anything to jam their finger into the metaphorical fast-forward button, eager to tip over the hourglass and hurry time along so they could just deal with the inevitable before their nerves completely immobilized them.

Enough dawdling, Alex thought, impatient and cagey. *I'm weary of sitting, meditating, thinking, overthinking and thinking again about the same things and my journey and these circumstances and Ryan and Kieran and everyone else. See? I'm rambling.*

CHAPTER 17

Even as Alex willed the time to pass, another half hour elapsed before Juneau arrived to greet them late that morning. They jumped at the door opening, startled even though they were anticipating her arrival. They got to their feet and waited for her command, but all she did was hurriedly wave them out the door, hold up her index and middle fingers, and whisper, "Come, we have two minutes."

After Juneau softly clicked Alex's former cell door shut behind them, they slunk down the dark corridor and to the right, just out of the atrium's sight. Alex saw two sets of eyes waiting for them; hopefully one of the pairs belonged to Xavier. As they tiptoed across the atrium toward that corridor, they felt more exposed than ever. After being locked in a cell for who knows how long, traversing such an open space felt unnatural, naked somehow. Revealing. Exposed. In the Panoptic's main atrium that boasted the central guard tower, they couldn't hide. One of the benefits of sitting in their cell was that they *could* hide, they *could* relish isolation from a world in which they continually felt subjected to oppressive forces. But they were very visible here, a fact which they hoped would go unnoticed if the tower guard were adequately distracted by Juneau's comrade. The Panoptic's atrium was much chillier than Alex's cell, causing goosebumps to break out across their arms and the back of their neck.

Once in the deserted corridor and out of sight of the tower, Juneau opened two cell doors. Her whispering evolved into rapid, urgent, breathless gasps. "Alex, Xavier, you know one another. This is Logan. They're helping us. Logan, you can trust Alex and Xavier; they're reliable."

Alex and Xavier had only a second to offer Logan a quick wave before Juneau yanked all three of them farther down the dim corridor. After double-checking the men's bathroom at the end of the hallway, she ushered them inside. "Change. Now. Hurry. I'll keep watch." She ducked back out into the hallway.

By luck of the draw, all the clothes Juneau left for them were "male" uniforms, ironically making Alex feel more comfortable in this decidedly anxious and uncertain situation. *Something as simple and fundamental as clothing can make or break one's self-confidence, even in times like these*, they thought.

Small, cobbled together team they may be, Alex noted a significant absence among the group, and it struck them almost to the point of tears that they hadn't processed the full weight of the gaping loss until that very moment: Ryan. Ryan would relish being a part of this scheme, the conspiracy and cunning of it all. Alex's denial of their separation folded under the gravity of not knowing exactly how long they'd been apart and the guilt in not having tried to make contact with him.

However, this was no time to cry over their losses. Filling each moment to the brim with action that would further their cause was essential. The three made quick work of stripping out of their prison garb, donning the freshly laundered uniforms, complete with American flag and FPNG insignia on each of the shoulders. They completed their ensembles with FPNG ball caps, which Juneau had instructed them to pull as far down over their eyes as possible. She had assured them that most of the guards were currently occupied at their posts in the tower, at the outer doors, or outside awaiting the rotting train and its new batch of cargo. Still, you can't be too careful.

The four slid like ghosts down hallway after hallway, some ablaze with those dreaded fluorescent lights Alex had come to loathe – always installed in school bathrooms, stark and clinical – with a burnt-out light here and there, neglected to be replaced.

Alex noted other signs of blatant building neglect: cracking concrete floors, walls, and mortar; exposed rebar; rusty hinges; long-ignored stains beneath their feet. They backtracked to the atrium and counterclockwise to the right, so they could emerge closer to the guard tower. Down another hallway and staircase, they then hung a right. Alex loved living in the shadows, on the periphery, far away from searching eyes. But this journey felt less like shelter and more like a rat's maze, the golden egg of escape eluding their grasp with every turn. The last thing they wanted to do was return to the atrium, not when they were so close to the outside world, maybe only four doors away. On their trek back from the bathroom, they forced one foot in front of the other, back into the trenches.

"Stick close now," Logan whispered behind them. Single file – Juneau, Logan, Xavier, and finally Alex – they wound their way upstream to the lion's den. The semicircle, from Alex's cell to the bathroom to reemerging across the atrium took maybe five minutes in total, but it felt like an eternity to Alex. As they reentered the Panoptic's main atrium, vast and breezy as they slunk through it, this nagging worry bled away as the totality of the present revolved in spirals around them and they focused their anxiety on one question: how much time did they have left to fly up the watchtower?

Alex observed the spiraling tower, gulped, sent up a vague prayer, and joined Juneau, Logan, and Xavier already ascending the rusting, squeaky spiral staircase to its top. *Maybe someone should have thought to oil this thing. For all the noise we're making, I may as well cry out, "Hey, shitheads! Over here! Incoming insurrection!"*

How had they not been detected yet? The group outside was probably in place, waiting. With no external signal, Alex could only hope that this was the right moment in which all the separate plans of the resistance would align, all the players in place, the singularity of the moment, the fulcrum on which progress would be turned.

These thoughts consumed Alex's mind, ascending step after step, *thunk* after *thunk*. They mentally repeated one word incessantly, one syllable with the right foot, the other with the left: *pro-gress, pro-gress, pro-gress*. After ten repetitions of *pro-gress*, Alex and company approached a door flanked by a series of wide windows the entire length of the central guard station. They all shifted into crouched positions around the door until Alex heard a cheery, "Come on in, Anderson!" *Is this the person who is expecting us?* Before they rushed the door and battered their way into the guard tower, Alex turned to note the dizzying Panoptic below them. They could have sworn they saw a couple of anticipatory gazes from folks still locked inside their cells below, watching the action unfold from their slim cell door windows.

A flurry of limbs, hats, nightsticks, and punches met Alex as they ran into the action and then immediately retreated to the periphery of the room with Xavier, unsure of what to do or who was battling it out in the throng. Their eyes shot directly to the switchboard, little pinpricks of light on small buttons dotting the whole thing, one for each prison cell, presumably.

Was this the plan? What the hell am I supposed to do? they wondered. They lost sight of Juneau in the struggle, but then saw her resurface, pinning her victim to the ground and strapping their hands behind their back with a zip tie. Juneau introduced her collaborator, Jamie, who had distracted the now-indisposed guard, and who now stood with a foot firmly planted on the guard's back.

"You're not going to hurt them anymore, are you?" Xavier probed tentatively.

Jamie smiled warmly, proclaimed their pronouns to be they/them/theirs, and said, "Oh, Brittany here? Brittany will be fine. No hard feelings, huh?"

Brittany struggled against the thick bandana tied around her mouth, only muffled grunts escaping in protest. Had she not been tackled and restrained, Alex had no doubt that Brittany *would* have had hard feelings, and would have alerted the nearest guard to the devious plot.

Jamie assured Xavier, "She'll be fine. No need for senseless violence, even in a case like this."

"Agreed," said Logan. "Now, let's do this."

Juneau wiped her brow, thick sweat glistening there, and tossed her hat and wig to the ground. *I knew it! There's no way Juneau would have chopped off her hair. I wondered how she'd kept it contained.* She pulled her voluminous hair into a tight bun. Alex thought Juneau looked like a queen just then, fiercely leading her troops into battle. The fiery determination burning in her eyes was evident and infectious. She exchanged knowing nods with Jamie and Alex, seeing how much they appreciated her and that they would eagerly follow her anywhere.

"So, what now?" Alex said, finally finding their voice for the first time since they stepped out of their cell.

"Let's hope the folks outside have created the distraction we need..." Juneau was interrupted by a blaring alarm emitted by every speaker in the Northeast Panoptic, including those on the side of the tower, sounding in five-second intervals. They heard the hurried shuffling of feet from outside the tower, and someone below shouted "All hands on deck!" The chaos brought a smile to Alex's face like nothing else had in weeks.

"And I think we're good," Juneau concluded.

"We won't be good for long," Alex reminded the group. "As long as we have the element of surprise on our side, we have a better shot, but we've got to maintain it."

Xavier looked nervous. "What do we do now? Wait? Go for it? Maintain our cover, or start releasing folks as soon as possible?"

Their hands already on the main cell switchboard, Jamie answered, "We do it now."

"Wait!"

"What, Alex?"

Recognizing that they had little time for sentiment, Alex cut to the heart of the matter. "Look, before we start this, I just have to say, thank you."

"What for, Alex?" Juneau asked.

"To you and Jamie, and even you two, as well." Alex looked Logan and Xavier each in the eyes with deep admiration. "Thank you for getting us here, for believing in us, for saving us. Let's get these assholes."

The look that fell across Juneau's face was one of pure friendship, admiration, and love. To hide the fact that they were on the verge of tears, Alex quickly hug-tackled Juneau. Jamie then retrieved the switchboard master key and shoved it into the circular red key shift at the head of the switchboard. A turn of the key lit an adjacent green button to life, indicating that the system was ready for the next command.

Alex looked back at the others, self-conscious about being the day's change agent, but knowing they had only a few moments of cover left to continue the coup. Xavier placed a hand on Alex's shoulder, nudging them forward. "It's all on you, Alex. Ready to pull the trigger?"

Alex punched their thumb into the green, pulsing button, and the board emitted a low beep. They gleefully skimmed their fingers across the tiny buttons, each representing a cell.

"Ready," they confirmed, and Alex ceremonially depressed each button one by one to unlock the cell doors. In confirmation, each little button switched from white to bright green. In their mind, Alex heard the *ch-clunks* of the cell locks releasing as they moved from one button to the next, from one person to the next.

"Maybe a little faster, Alex," urged Juneau, rotating her wrist in circles to goad them on. Alex punched the buttons faster until half of them were green. As they did so, a thought nagged at the back of Alex's mind, messing with their concentration. While their eyes were singularly focused on the switchboard, they failed to look through the glass and into the wider Panoptic atrium. "This may seem like an obvious problem that y'all planned for, but do these folks know they can and *should* leave? Like, we're unlocking the doors, but that doesn't automatically open them. They'll hear the clicks, but…"

Xavier slung his arm across Alex's shoulders. "See for yourself," he said with a wide smile. "I'll take over." Xavier nudged Alex over to replace them as they paced to the window. Their mouth dropped open because what they saw were, well, flocks.

Flocks of people still dressed in their black, Panoptic-issued uniforms, trotting in roiling waves toward the leftmost side of the atrium where the maze of corridors led to the harsh outdoors. Confused eyes blinked and widened in shock from behind some of the cell doors, but in a domino effect, they saw people leave and realized they could, too. Those folks then fled and inspired another wave to do the same, over and over until Alex saw almost every cell door open and its inhabitants make a break for it. Alex didn't know most of these people, but they sure did care about each and every one getting out. Alex was fishing for a "coming out" metaphor, but they were too amped up to think clearly.

They watched as Xavier pushed the very last cell release button. "That's it," he said. "They're all open. Now what?"

"We're in for the fight of our lives, let's go!" Juneau called with enthusiasm. Brittany was still tied up, yelling muffled threats and causing enough of a commotion for Jamie to return and plant her back down against the wall farthest from the switchboard.

Alex noticed Jamie's huffs and gasps as they fought Brittany to the ground, but like a homing beacon trained on its treasure, Alex caught a glimpse of a fiery-blue, curly head of hair in the atrium and froze on the spot. The sighting was remarkable, like spotting a vibrant peacock in the middle of a stark, white tundra. Alex blinked hard once, and again, and again and again until both the blinking and guttural disbelief of who they were seeing showered them in disbelief. *It couldn't be. It can't be.*

"Alex?" Juneau's tone was pleading; their window was closing and it was time to flee. She tugged on Alex's shoulder with serious insistence. "Alex, let's go! Now!"

"No. I mean, yes. Hold on."

"What? What's come over you? What did you see?" Juneau leaned over the field of green buttons as well, diving her eyes into the thick crowds to identify any anomaly. "What's the deal? Hello?"

Holy shit. A wash of both relief and dread drained down Alex's body. *But how?* "I just saw someone that… I haven't seen in forever. I can't believe it… how could they…?"

"Who, Alex?" Juneau and Xavier asked in unison.

"It's not Ryan, is it?" Juneau said. "That would be impossible."

Alex shook their head too hard. "No, no, for heaven's sake, Ryan's not here. Look! Curly blue hair! It's Kieran."

"Who?" Xavier pried again.

"Does someone want to tell me what the hell is going on?" Alex yelled, rife with confusion and hurt, and feeling their cool slipping away with every moment of silence from Juneau and Jamie. "Clearly I'm missing something."

Juneau almost laughed, which Alex found super inappropriate given the urgency and incredulity of the situation. Her tone was one of relief. "Oh yeah, Kieran."

Alex's eyes narrowed in deep suspicion. "Why don't you sound surprised by that? How do you know Kieran? They were just this guy… uh, person I met on vacation. There's no logical reason they would be here or know you."

"Listen quickly, Alex. I know. I know all of this, and I know Kieran. Well, I know *of* Kieran. Word came that they talked to one of Shay's coworkers shortly after your arrest. They volunteered to be one of the last batch of prisoners brought into the Panoptic before the escape."

Even if I were to believe that, to accept the surreality of her statement... "What? No way. Well, why are they *in here*, then? I thought everyone else was outside?"

Juneau shrugged, unsure. "Maybe they came in to help others escape." Directing their searching eyes back out onto the crowd, Alex did recall from their brief glimpse that Kieran was wearing street clothes, not prison garb like the rest.

"Why in the hell did they do that? They had a good deal, living in a small town. Easier to hide. Why screw that up?"

Juneau rolled her eyes. "Ugh, it's so obvious. Don't you know, Alex? The answer is right here."

"What? Where?"

"You."

"Me? What?"

"Jeez, Alex, it's not difficult to put together. Kieran is here for *you*."

"Why me?"

She dished them another sarcastic roll of her eyes. "Seriously? How can you be so intuitive and so thick all at once, Alex? Especially when it comes to feelings and affection. Kieran so obviously has feelings for you."

"Enough chit chat! I will shove each and every one of you out this door and push you down those stairs if it gets you moving!" Jamie shouted, shepherding the group out the watchtower door. They sandwiched Alex between Xavier and Logan and pushed them all along. Alex noticed that Logan hadn't spoken much at all since meeting outside their cells earlier that morning.

"You okay?" they asked Logan, who answered with a silent nod. "I've been involved in this for a while, Alex. I just want it to be done."

"You and me both. We've got your back."

"Likewise."

Clung, clung, clung, clung. The quintet rushed down the steep tower staircase and into the hoard, where many people were still wading their way out of the Panoptic, some still shuffling along at a confused trot, others full-out sprinting toward the exit. Alex heard that blasted alarm again, once relatively muffled by the walls of the watchtower, now voluminous in its echo off the rotunda's walls. It reminded Alex of Jo's morning phone alarm, which began as a soft beeping and quickened its pace to that of a roaring, racing heartbeat until Jo finally shut the damn thing off. Alex recalled their former life in a vicious flashback as they ran in sync with the black-clad tide of prisoners flooding their way through several atrium doorways and hopefully into the relative safety and freedom of Mount Washington's summit. Alex scanned the room to find a window through which they could gauge the weather outside, but no dice. No idea what they were running into. Alex projected another vague, silent prayer into the ether, hoping it would reach the ears of some favorable deity. They now felt the beeping alarm beating their eardrums, and they crammed their fingers into them to try to thwart the pounding. *I just want to get out of here as fast as possible. Maybe I'll see Kieran outside. I can't find them so I'm sure they're gone.*

I still can't believe that they're here. Why didn't Juneau tell me? She knew about the entirety of the plot, so what could have been the harm? Did she think I would split? Break my promise at the first sign of Kieran and leave my role unfulfilled?

I won't believe that Kieran is here until I see them once again. Where are they?

Juneau? Xavier? Logan? Now I can't find them either. Blast these crowds.

And then the alarm cut out.

A speaker crackled to life like nails on a chalkboard, the volume turned up twenty times beyond that of a normal broadcast. Whatever it was that Officer Paine was saying bled into the background as Alex finally located Kieran, wonderful, beautiful Kieran. They were opening the last two ground floor cell doors and ushering their occupants out into the swelling tide of bodies.

"Kieran." Alex thought they merely said it, a tiny word lost in the cacophonous chaos, but then Kieran looked directly at them. Alex could have screamed it for all they knew, but all that mattered in that moment was that Kieran was here with them. Kieran looked as if they were boring their eyes into Alex's, but they suddenly spun their head around to continue searching for the source of their name. Kieran turned away, so Alex sprinted at them. The tide kicked and threw Alex here and there, and they thrashed their way past the folks left in the Panoptic and the guards in their midst.

Guards? Wait, what? Are they coming back to claim the Panoptic? They must know something is afoot by now.

The thought swam in one ear and out the other as they collided with Kieran and into an open cell. They clutched to Kieran's acid-washed jean jacket like a life raft in a torrential riptide. Kieran began to bat in wild gesticulations at Alex, thinking they were someone else, but Alex reached their hands up, held Kieran's face to theirs, and they sunk to the ground together, crumpling limb after limb as they folded into one another in relief.

CHAPTER 18

Alex so desperately wanted their first words to Kieran to be meaningful, kind, unforgettable, romantic. Even a simple and affectionate "hi" would have sufficed. Instead, they slapped Kieran's bicep a bit harder than they'd intended and shouted, "Why in all hell did you come here?" But the tears in Kieran's eyes, their flushed face, and their heavy, panting breaths all made Alex want to kiss them, so they did.

Kieran stole Juneau's very words from her mouth, remarking with laughter, "Alex, you are so thick sometimes." In lieu of playfully flicking Alex on the forehead, Kieran kissed them on the head instead. Drawing them both back to the situation at hand, Kieran blew out a long sigh, collected themselves, and dragged both of them to their feet. "More time for catching up and sentimentality later, babe. Let's get the hell out of here."

"Right." Alex's fly-or-die instinct kicked into overdrive and they fantasized about sprouting wings and soaring over the crowd, through the top of the rotunda, and leaving an Alex-and-Kieran-sized hole in the ceiling. Only once they were in the clouds would they turn back and watch the rest crumble behind them.

The sound of shuffling feet, squeaking shoes, and yelling interrupted Alex's thoughts as folks called to one another and rushed out of the atrium. A brief hush followed before screaming ensued, guttural, frightened, animal-like screaming reverberating off the rotunda. Alex and Kieran rose to their full heights in unison to see what seemed like every remaining Panoptic guard converging on the atrium. Officer Paine lead the battle formation, grabbing and handing off as many prisoners as he could to his subordinates, who threw their thrashing bodies into empty cells. With horror and a wash of sweat drenching their back, Alex locked eyes with Officer Paine, who obviously recognized them from intake day and from his interruption in their cell, almost foiling the well-harbored escape plan. Paine dropped the person he'd twisted into an arm bar and started for Alex and Kieran, his pounding footsteps getting closer and closer, matching the rhythmic pumps of Alex's own heartbeat. Alex tugged on Kieran, who saw Paine, too, and they bolted, leaping over unconscious guards and a few stragglers caught in the Foundation's last-ditch effort to retain control of as many prisoners as they could claw back into their cells.

As they rushed toward the exit, only a few guards impeding their progress to freedom, Alex thought ahead to the next moment, and the next, and the next until they had a roughly formed plan should they escape this place with relative safety.

From another month, another year, another lifetime, it seemed, Alex recalled being in this very same position with Ryan, rushing for the door of the Sanford Sawmill to escape the FPNG's clutches. They had run headfirst into the pouring rain, embracing it and allowing it to fuel their bodies as they ran for their lives in the midst of a nor'easter. Escape after escape, close call after close call. This escape was just another iteration.

My life seems to be pockmarked with escapes: escape from the sawmill, escape from Principal Hatchett, momentary escape from arrest. Yet no escape from binary society. Will I be ever able to set aside my penchant for escaping?

Despite the brief proactive plan Alex formulated, it went to shit as soon as Alex was snagged by a guard they hadn't detected from their periphery as they rushed for the exit. He reeled Alex back into the Panoptic when they were a measly foot from the outside world. Alex wildly punched and writhed, even attempting to bite their attacker. The guard had to stop a few times to readjust their hold on Alex, a fisherman reforming his stance to wind in the day's prize catch, but this guard had so little meat on him that he could barely retain his tenuous grasp on Alex. It was on the third iteration of these breaks to adjust his grip that the guard called for help. Alex waited for the pause, and then firmly swished their wrist in a counterclockwise move to break the guard's hold on one hand, then another, kicked the guard in the crotch, used the resulting momentum to propel themselves out of the door, shouldered past Kieran, and landed so as to sprint until their lungs burned and their legs gave away. *Thanks for inviting me to that self-defense class during Buddy Week, Juneau. I owe you one.*

The mountaintop's snow-dusted tendrils of wind gripped Alex at the threshold of the Panoptic's entryway, embracing their entire body and those of their friends around them in a hug that dragged them into their entropic present. The absolute howl of Mount Washington's wind unleashed itself and imparted an impression of the mountain as a mourning, ravenous, raging beast, cheated of its dinner just as the Panoptic was of its prisoners. Alex almost lost their breath, not only because of the shards of cold, unforgiving, pre-winter air cutting the insides of their throat as they inhaled it, but because of the panoramic view stretching itself out for their eyes to drink in.

Alex remarked on the disk-shaped wall cloud that inched its way from the distant horizon over to Mount Washington's summit, moments from eclipsing the mountain completely; its puffy condensation ran in concentric arcs to round out its rotund circumference. Aside from the encroaching wall cloud, the remainder of the earth's ceiling stayed a calm, sky blue, clear snowy peaks from the Presidential range's other mountains almost as blinding as car headlights on a stormy night. Watching this massive cloud sift over their head, Alex felt like a small, inconsequential being on the massive mountain on which they stood, fragile in comparison to the grand scale of every landmark around them. Alex wished they could stop and stare at the thing, watching the weight of the cloud's darkness eclipse their periphery and the extent of their eyesight.

The sublimity of the landscape struck Alex like a speeding train, and they drank in every inch as they reduced their sprint to a cautious run to account for the five inches of slippery light snow on the summit. The view shifted slightly as they ran, Kieran in hand.

At a particularly rocky crag that marked one edge of the summit, and from which the railroad tracks descended down the mountainside, Alex slid to a stop and looked around to take stock of their current status. There was one guard off in the distance, in the Panoptic's massive entryway, and more would certainly arrive soon. Alex squinted against the snow's glare, and as the sun slipped behind a cloud, they saw pinpricks of people dotting the mountainside.

"So, what's the plan now?" they asked, their icy breath billowing from their body like smoke from a disgruntled dragon's snarling maw. Darting their eyes around, they realized, "Wait, where's the fence?"

Speaking with a voice hoarse from yelling and exhausted from running, Kieran doubled over and breathlessly replied, "There was a fence?"

"How did I not notice when I arrived? There's no fence around this place, no protective perimeter."

"You mean like an electric fence? No way. I honestly don't think there ever was one, Alex."

"Why?"

"Probably because the Foundation didn't account for prison breaks when they built this place atop a mountain. It's dangerous and frigid – who would willingly run out into this?"

"Alex! Over here! Hurry!" Alex whipped around to see Juneau gesturing wildly, and a small crew around her rounding up as many people as they could gather. Granting themselves one last look at the wretched Panoptic, they saw guards in white snowsuits and battle gear spilling out from its dastardly insides. Alex spat into the snow in their direction in lieu of shooting a middle finger, then they grabbed Kieran's hand, and half-ran, half-trudged toward Juneau. After such an arduous morning, they were beginning to tire from the effort and were losing feeling in the tips of their toes and fingers to the biting chill.

Snow tangled Alex's loose hair and, with no jacket, they were shivering violently. Kieran offered them their jean jacket, but Alex refused, not wanting to stop. At first, Alex assumed from the sharp flakes cutting their cheeks that it was snowing again, but a quick look confirmed that it was just the wind whipping residual snow from the summit's frigid ground. Across the Presidential mountain range, Alex saw a lip of blue sky, and hoped they'd be able to survive until that blue sky eclipsed them. When Kieran and Alex finally reached Juneau, Juneau threw Alex an extra guard coat she'd been carrying and they swiftly put it on and replied, "Where to?"

"Follow me. Quickly, everyone."

Treading at Juneau's heels, Alex felt relatively safe. Ironically, trekking across an open mountainside, Alex felt more secure than being stowed away in a cell or cordoning themselves off in their room back in Springfield. Perhaps it was the comfort of nature, the anonymity of the wilderness in which two strangers can simply smile, nod, and then resume their respective solitary travels. This anonymity comforted Alex, being able to own who they were without keeping others at an arm's length. Perhaps it was also the relief that, even though most of this group were strangers, Alex knew they weren't alone. These outcasts were all forging similar paths. In that thought, humans are comfortably predictable.

I've nothing to lose now, and maybe a new life to gain, Alex mused.

As they scaled farther down the side of Mount Washington, dense thickets and small, bony trees donning grand sweaters of snowfall greeted them. Only a leaf here and there remained on the trees' husky skeletons, and a painful longing for the summer and fall seasons wracked Alex. Adding insult to injury was the annoying height of the snow, enough to inhibit swift progress down the mountainside, and more than substantial enough to leave tracks in their wake. The trees continuously shed their snow on their head and shoulders, as if they couldn't care less how much Alex already had to bear today. Alex knew there was an intended destination, but they were unsure of where and when their ragtag, motley crew would arrive. The trek reminded Alex of a more brutal iteration of writing a long story when you know it's nearing completion; the ending is not quite in sight, the loose threads of unsewn character development and plot still dangling, not yet tied up in a publishable fashion. Yet, to finish, the writer must trudge through the necessary words and pages nonetheless – so damn close that your acute senses can detect the ending and the long rest awaiting you afterward. But, in the meantime, you have to diligently write your way to the conclusion.

Juneau detected that the group was slowing down, so she pleaded, "I know the descent is difficult; we're all exhausted, but you must keep moving." Alex didn't quite feel like talking, trying instead to process the last hour and maintain steady breathing in the thin air. But they did hear Jamie, walking in the front of the pack, ask, "Juneau, how many folks do we have here?"

"Twenty-three," she answered, eyes ahead and trained on their destination. *Does Juneau know where she is going? Do we even have a plan or are we wandering aimlessly? Are she and Jamie making this up as they go along? With everyone's lives at stake, I sincerely hope not.*

"And the others?"

"No clue," Juneau admitted. "Hopefully, they were able to rendezvous with other groups, maybe with Shay's or at base camp."

Base camp? So, she does have a destination in mind.

"Here's hoping." Kieran spoke for the first time since the start of their trek, wading their way to the front of the group. "Have you guys seriously thought this through?"

Juneau's irritation was evident in her tense, bristly replies. "Yes, Kieran. Believe it not, we have."

"Care to share?"

"Kieran, hush," Alex tried to shush them, but Kieran continued to push.

"Sorry if I seem cross; I'd just like to know the game plan here. I'm sure I'm not alone in feeling left out in the dark from your little core circle here." Alex looked around to gauge the collective reaction of the group. Many meek nods followed, including from Logan and Xavier, who quietly said, "Yeah, same."

Juneau spun around, walking backward through the heavy snow. Index finger over her mouth to shush the group, she whispered, but the howling wind threatened to stifle her words. "Please, keep moving. We're descending the mountainside another fifteen hundred feet in altitude. The faster we move, the sooner we arrive; it's hard to say when, but my goal is to move safely and steadily. There's a camp, our camp. It's critically important that we're unseen and not followed, or we risk exposing the scope of our cause and resources. The camp, our summer location, is so far up the mountainside and remote that we aren't exposed to passersby, but it's also far enough away from the Panoptic to escape their detection."

Another liminal space, Alex noted. "That's a dangerous line to toe."

"You're right about that, Alex, which is why it's so critical that we get there…"

"ANDERSON! ANDERSON!"

Juneau froze, as did Alex, which resulted in Kieran and a few others colliding into them and into one another. A small chorus of "Oofs" and "Oh craps" and hushing gasps followed. A couple of folks stumbled into the snow. The call was unmistakable: it was Officer Paine. Alex didn't even have to turn around to recognize his voice. Their escape, not without its challenges, had gone much more seamlessly than Alex had predicted.

Who else would it be? Paine has been a thorn in my side from the start. Too easy, they scoffed to themselves. *Once you've conquered one fight, there's always another to challenge you. Why is he out here? Why would he want to pursue us? Is he hell-bent on reclaiming as many prisoners as he can? Or does he have his sights set on capturing his once-loyal guard, J. Anderson?*

Officer Paine's voice sounded as if it were just a few feet away; the low, bare vegetation characteristic of such high altitudes, wearing little but snow, lacked the muffling power that the larger evergreens farther down the hillside offered. Camouflage would be equally as sparse. Escaping down this patchy, balding mountaintop would be like threading the eye of a needle.

Silent hand gestures from Juneau had them trotting down the icy, rocky hillside once again, slipping and sliding, until Alex discovered a wide outcropping that jutted off the mountain, supported by a boulder beneath. The windfall offered a relatively large, concave hiding place with sheltering boulders on either side. Unlike the crest of the summit, the snow here was patchy, brown grass bleeding out from under the sparse coating – perfect for hiding footsteps. A few sister hiding spaces spotted the surrounding land. Recognizing that this was one of the most feasible hiding spots around, the group of twenty plus folks crammed themselves together and faded into Mount Washington's background.

Not a second too soon. Heavy, crunching footfalls invaded the brief silence, quick and insistent at first, then slowing, cautious, sensing for flight or movement. Paine paced back and forth across the back of the craggy crescent that safeguarded Juneau, Alex, Jamie, Kieran, and Xavier, first one way, then another, then doubling back to survey the area again. Alex marked his progress as the crunchy steps from the snow above softened when he stepped upon the grassy frost near their hiding space. Unlike Paine's slowing pace, Alex's heartbeat hammered away, fearful for the moment he eclipsed the front of the crag's underbelly and discovered them.

But to Alex's extreme surprise, Paine retreated from the edge of the crag. He paused above their heads, and Alex quietly clapped a hand over their mouth to muffle their breathing. The slightest tell could give them away.

A scream and a harried call for backup farther up the side of the mountain punctuated the deafening pause. So, Paine left, and Alex could breathe once again.

PART 3

THE VISIBLE SPECTRUM

CHAPTER 19

The rolling clouds are delicious, resembling milk chocolate Swiss Rolls tumbling their way across the sky to eclipse our makeshift campsite, Alex thought. The sun rimmed the clouds' underbelly, and against their darkness, the evergreens and the few trees with sparse leaves still remaining were radiant. The scene was beautiful, but Alex soon lost focus, their thoughts drifting to disbelief at their recent success.

The FPNG won't overlook an entire prison break, they knew.

Decadent, rich, and witchy, Alex took one last look at the landscape before resolutely closing the tent flap against the next barrage of wind. The anticipated wave of leaves roiled over the heads of Alex and Kieran; the leaves' feathery, soft flutters grazed the tent's smooth, weather-resistant, green exterior. Wisps of windy tendrils hugged the tent, and the supple sounds brought Alex back to the frothy seaside once again. These leaves would be the last of the season, leaving the bare mountainside exposed with the remaining raw, ribbed branches. The natural energy of the moment captured Alex like a spiritual, Samhain, or Halloween ritual: organic and sacred.

Alongside Juneau, Jamie, Kieran, and the rest of their new friends, they had sat for an additional half hour under that crag, to ensure Paine wasn't smoking them out. But when Kieran peeked out with a hesitant eye from around a boulder, nothing but a fresh wave of wind greeted them, stinging their eyes. The sharp, frozen smell in the air was laced with new snow. And so, they journeyed onward once again, exhausted and treading with heavy limbs that reminded Alex of when you get out of a pool after hours of play; it feels like the earth's gravity itself changes.

They trudged for two and a half more hours, on and on as the clouds grew heavier with every footfall.

Upon arriving at camp, their apparent end destination, Alex thought it was deserted until a few stragglers emerged from tents and firesides, maintaining the area and holding down the fort for those stationed in the Panoptic. A dozen or so tents were spread out within a particularly dense copse of trees, still bearing some snow. Complementing the tents were four fire pits, only one of which was lit.

Juneau said, "This is the rendezvous point. Whoever makes it out will meet us back here."

"We're the first ones back?" asked Alex.

"Yep, seems that way." The voice came from the person sitting by the closest fire, fueling the central flame by redistributing wood and paper in the pit with a poker. Earmuffs adorned their head over their asymmetrical undercut, the rest of their hair in a fishtail braid down their back. They wore black eyeliner and had a wonderfully low, soothing voice. As the pack of escapees joined this person at the fire, Juneau ran to give them a warm bear hug. The visceral smell of fresh kindling reinvigorated Alex, even for how tired they felt. The smell was one of comfort and security. Kieran smelled like that, too, faintly.

"Hey, Kaya. Any news?"

"Nope," Kaya replied. "Like I said, you're the first ones back. Hopefully, more are coming soon. Until then, get warm and make yourselves comfortable. We have spare clothes, boots, and coats."

"Right behind ya!"

Alex whipped around for the source of the call, not recognizing the voice at first. They felt panicked that it was an FPNG official, having stalked the group there.

But it was Shay, of all people, with twenty or so folks in tow. The sheer surprise and excitement of seeing Shay again took over and Alex ran full tilt at her. Maybe it was her infectious confidence, or her connection to Ryan, or maybe Alex was just relieved to see her alive.

"Alex, oh my God!"

"How are you? How have you been?"

"Shitty until now, but now I feel amazing. I can't believe it!"

Juneau joined the welcoming party and slung an arm around Alex's shoulders. "You'd be so proud of them, Shay. Alex, Xavier, and Logan were integral parts of our escape plan. They helped us take the guard tower."

"No friggin way!"

"Wait, why did you ask me to help? Why would my assistance be necessary if Shay was there to fill the role, too?" asked Alex.

Juneau responded, "Why are you questioning my decision in choosing you?"

Shay shut them down. "Much more time to catch up later, but I'm so happy y'all are safe! Are you the first group back?"

"Yes," Kaya and Juneau said in unison.

"Well, we'll see who else arrives. How many do you reckon we can accommodate here?" Shay asked.

"Not the capacity of the entire Panoptic, that's for sure. We tried to group people as efficiently as possible, but this camp was only intended to accommodate about sixty people."

"And the other camps? Could they accommodate more?"

"Only if we have a few folks to spare for supply runs, but I'm not sure about our remaining resources and supplies – tents, food, and warm clothing. We'd need to spare a few for reconnaissance to ensure the FPNG aren't scoping out these areas."

"I have a solution for that," Shay interjected.

"Do tell," Kieran said. Alex almost jumped, forgetting Kieran was behind them.

Shay replied, "I will, don't worry. I want to ensure that everyone knows what's happening next, or rather, that we collectively decide what we want to happen next. I want to sit tight until tomorrow to see how many folks arrive, and take it from there. Sound like a plan?"

"Definitely." Kieran seemed satisfied enough.

"Tomorrow it is," Juneau said. "For now, let's get comfy. Kaya, are you willing to share the camp's rations with these folks?"

"Absolutely. I hope y'all like beans and rice."

After pitching in to cook the meal, the group settled into their tents. Alex found themselves here, with Kieran, finally alone for the first time since Alex smashed into them in the chaos of the Northeast Panoptic prison break. It felt weird to have this type of intimate privacy with someone else again. Aside from Juneau's sporadic visits, the occasional vent conversation with Xavier, the horrific reeducation sessions, and mealtimes, Alex had nothing but endless time alone in their cell, time to think. To enjoy intimate company with just one other person felt foreign. They were grateful for the time, but it also made Alex cognizant of how much they missed Ryan, and how they cherished their frequent one-on-one time that only best friends could appreciate.

Catching themselves contemplating all this and recalling the Swiss Roll clouds once again, they shook their head to draw themselves back into the present conversation that had died as soon as Alex had spaced out into the mountainside. They admitted, "I get drunk on storms."

Kieran smiled knowingly. "You're the only person I know who loves fall more than I do," Kieran chuckled with an amused grin. "If and when I grow my hair out, I'd let this wind whip it around all day long. It seems glamorous. Very aesthetic."

"Haha yeah, until the wind twists your hair into a rat's nest, like mine."

"Please, you couldn't look like a rat's nest if you tried, Alex."

"Clearly, you haven't known me for very long."

"Long enough to know that I like you very much," said Kieran, and they bridged the gap between their body and Alex's with a long, tender kiss that made Alex flush below the belt.

"How are you so damn seductive?" they asked.

Kieran tipped an imaginary hat at Alex. "I learn from the best."

"Kieran, how I feel about you is… complicated. I owe you honesty. Despite that confusion, I'm damn elated that you're here. With me."

Kieran's expression was one of genuine shock and confusion. "Why complicated? Because of my pronoun screw-up on our last date in Springfield?"

Alex frowned and nodded their head in unfortunate agreement. "Yes. But if I'm being truthful, I also have a sneaking, dreadful suspicion that your uncle reported me, that he was the catalyst behind my arrest." They expected Kieran to be more offended than they were when they replied.

"Do you have any reason to believe he would have?"

"Well, do you have any reason to believe he would *not*?" Alex countered, brushing their fingers against Kieran's prickly facial hair, imagining how similar scruff would feel on their own face. *In some sense, our bodies send a message to others about who we are, or at least, who strangers think we are. That is, unless we're robbed of our agency and have no control over how we can present ourselves,* Alex thought. *Even if we could, would we? Why is self-love and acceptance so radical?*

"So, what are we doing, Alex? I've endured too many vague relationships in my short life, and I desperately don't want this one to fall into that same pattern."

"We're here, right now. You and me. I want you, Kieran, exclusively. But there's something I – we – need to do first."

"And what is that?"

"Fight back." Kieran rolled their eyes, to which Alex replied with an equally questioning look. "What's that for?"

"Obviously, I want to fight back, but we need the whole damn plan first. I want transparency from Juneau and the others, the higher-ups."

"Kieran, there are no higher-ups here."

"You insist as much with such ease, but there *are* evident leaders, the keepers of the collective knowledge about this scheme, our decisions, our plan. We all got told bits and pieces of the plan to play our respective parts, but I want the whole dang thing."

Alex rubbed Kieran's arm to comfort them. "I don't believe that Juneau or Jamie or Shay or whoever would willingly deprive us of vital information. If they did any of that, it was to safeguard the mission's integrity."

"Or to keep us in the dark," Kieran said, bitterness evident in their tone, and they dodged their glance away to the tent's entrance, avoiding Alex's.

Alex sighed and tried another tactic. "It does feel that way, yes, but I doubt it's a hierarchical thing. We're trying to dismantle that, remember?"

"I know, but it doesn't feel that way." Kieran maintained their dark expression.

"If you feel that way, let's step up."

"I have stepped up!"

Alex softened their hold on Kieran and spoke gently. "You have. I know you have. Thank you for coming back for me." Alex leaned back in and placed a warm hand on Kieran's upper thigh. One kiss led to another and another until Alex faltered, retreated, and asked, "Is this okay?"

"Absolutely."

Kieran kissed further and further down Alex's body, tracing winding roads with their lips, no defined destination in sight, exploring Alex's lips and then their neck, their belly. Kieran drew themselves back up to Alex's face as Alex started to squirm and buck their hips.

Kieran asked, "Are you okay?"

"Mmmmm," was Alex's bare reply, unlocking Kieran's belt in response. "Feels nice."

"Just wait."

"But what about you?"

"No," Kieran insisted. "You first." Alex loved hearing those words and knew they could get accustomed to them, to hearing those the words *and* to Kieran sticking around.

CHAPTER 20

The following morning, Alex and Kieran did something they'd been deprived of for almost their entire lives: they donned clothes that made them feel euphoric. They'd both sifted through the clothing Kaya had offered them, choosing matching jeans and faded buffalo plaid, wool shirts – blue for Alex, yellow for Kieran – and Alex added a puffy vest to the ensemble for extra warmth. Lacking proper shoes, Alex was stuck with the pair from their Panoptic prison uniform, but at least they felt warmer, more protected from the elements. Emerging from their tent, Alex thanked the gods that the day wasn't as freezing as the previous afternoon during their teeth-chattering escape. Still, Alex guessed the temperature was in the high thirties Fahrenheit.

Alex had looked down at their body as they changed, no mirror in sight. Their nonbinary body, nonbinary in its own right and in Alex's right to declare it as such. Sure, they'd like some more body hair – more stubble, in particular – and definitely some changes to their downstairs region, but all in all, this body was theirs, and they were proud of it: proud of the random gray freckle on their left hand, of their dimples when they smiled wide, of the little red "sun spot" freckles dotting their hairline. In some ways, Alex wouldn't trade this body for anything, or for anyone. Alex was firm in the opinion that they weren't so much born in the wrong body, as it was that external powers were enforcing the wrong *things* and *expectations* upon their body. Should they talk to Kieran about it, they were sure Kieran would agree. This was the unheard narrative. So many platforms are given to folks who reduce gender to body, and who tout that the only way to be trans, by FPNG standards, was to assume the "born in the wrong body" storyline. Alex realized that not everyone identifies with that mainstream story. Not Alex, and not Kieran, certainly.

Hand in hand, Alex and Kieran joined the small group of folks around a fire pit just two tents away, cooking eggs and, you guessed it, more beans. Alex met Kieran's eyes with an apologetic smile, which

Kieran silently chuckled at; Alex loved beans, but they'd accidentally farted on Kieran a couple of times when they were sleeping last night.

Shay patted the end of the blanketed rock beside her and motioned for Alex to take a seat, with a hushed, "Good morning!" Kieran sat on Shay's other side and took over for her at the skillet, flipping the fried eggs like a pro.

"Anyone else awake?" Alex whispered.

Shay nodded. "A few other people murmuring and stirring in their tents, but you're the first to breakfast. Feel free to take an egg and some beans before they're all gone."

"Thanks." Alex noticed the frost-covered tents in the purple morning light; a cloud-free sky and bright sun promised a chilly but clear day. "Looks like the storm blew over. I thought it would set in for a day or two."

"Same, but looks like it blew to the other side of the mountain. Maybe the Panoptic got dumped on before it flew away." Her lighthearted laugh was pure and satisfying, considering the very different, more serious tones they had assumed back at the nonbinary support group, the one Alex had barely survived. "Still, we're far from being in the clear, especially in this mountain range."

"True. Have you guys tented during snowstorms and blizzards like this before?"

"You bet, but not often and I haven't personally. There are a couple of safe houses around here, believe it or not. So those of us who inhabit the area year-round live out here as long as they can and hunker down when need be. The camping season all depends on when the frost and first snow arrive, or if more than a few people are sick." Shay sniffed up some snot of her own, before continuing. "I probably shouldn't be out here for too long, myself."

"How many people live up here full time?"

"I'm not quite sure, Alex. I'm not acquainted with everyone, but I'd estimate a hundred or so, between those that occupy safehouses in the country and those who keep to themselves. That's just this area, remember. There's more of us scattered around northern New England. Surely, there are groups like ours everywhere, but again, that's just my best guess."

"You said you had a plan?" Glancing over at Kieran, Alex switched gears and asked the question before they could.

"I do. I'll give you the teaser version. My Gran lives not too far from here."

"Where?"

"In a town called Bartlett. She's retired and lives on a farm that she and her partner run. She's got land, a sizeable farmhouse, a substantial food supply from her livestock and chickens, a huge barn – shelter and protection."

"So, you're saying we should all trek there? Would your Gran have us?"

"She definitely would. She told me long ago that my friends and I are always welcome, day or night. She knows who I am and she's proud of me, wants to protect me, and has always been a rock. If she knew about you, Kieran, all of us, she'd want to extend that protection to y'all, as well."

"Shay, I'm sure that when she said that, she wasn't extending the proverbial invite to you and fifty of your closest friends, or however many of us there are. Speaking of which, how many came in last night?"

"Another thirty or so. People are crammed into the available tent space right now, as you can imagine."

"Yikes, yeah. Time to move on soon?" Alex asked. Kieran nodded along with them, absorbing the details.

"Absolutely," Shay answered. "But before we do, I want to check in with everyone. See what the consensus is. See how everyone's feeling. From what I can tell, there were relatively few casualties."

"Who *were* the casualties?" Kieran always felt the need to examine the difficult issues. For now, Alex preferred to abide by Thomas Gray's poem, "Ode on a Distant Prospect of Eton College." He wrote, "Thought would destroy their paradise no more; Ignorance is bliss."

But Kieran's right, they thought. *Wasn't it I who was probing Juneau about our macro-level plan? Pushing her to entertain the possibility of demolishing other Panoptica and the repercussions of not doing so? Of letting our fellows suffer as we rest on our own laurels?*

Juneau was correct, however, in knowing that we have to take this process one step at a time, to first assess our current situation and then pave a path forward so we have the ability to accomplish more in the future.

Shay shuffled uneasily, dishing out the beans and eggs to distract herself. "I don't know."

"Why not?" The trio jumped at Logan's unexpected interruption. Alex was sure that Logan's stealth had earned their space on Juneau's "breakout" team, or whatever she called it. Alex's heart thumped wildly in their chest, and for a microsecond, their flight instinct had kicked in and they stood ready to flee.

"Jesus, Logan." Alex turned to face them head-on and Logan met them with a tired, disgruntled stare, brow furrowed as low as it would go.

"So?" Logan persisted.

Shay stood. "It's time to talk."

***

They finally sat down to talk at dusk. For how utterly drained Alex felt, how they slumped into a sitting position with every chance they got, they thought it a crime the time was likely only 4:30 p.m. Even though they did very little that day aside from huddle at firesides for small meals and attend that fleeting meeting in the morning, the wintry darkness and cold had sapped what little energy did remain, as it does to many folks as the winter solstice approaches.

It feels like it should be midnight. Alex wished they could bypass this next meeting of the minds for bed, though they knew that their attendance was critical. Based on Logan's sullen mood earlier, Alex had a sneaking suspicion that the conversation was going to be a tad uncomfortable.

Along with Kieran, who rubbed Alex's back to warm them up, Juneau, Shay, Logan, and a few others took seats around the central-most, crackling, flamboyant fire. Everyone at camp gathered around, splayed out in a loose circle around the firelight. Alex stood to take in the scene, head after head, person after person. They marveled at the group of survivors gathered there. Eyes probing, eyes wondering, eyes bold, eyes angry, eyes startled and scared and every emotion in the spectrum. A wash of immense pride washed over Alex, and they felt an inexplicable love for each and every human before them, honored to be in the presence of such courageous, fearless, and big-hearted people. These folks felt just as much like Alex's family now as their biological one; they had a new, communal family. Their smile might have been muddled by the shadows cast by the ever-changing flames, but they smiled out at everyone nonetheless before taking a seat.

Exuding confidence and authority, Juneau stood up and took Alex's place, jumping up on the one free spot on the log Alex and Kieran shared, prepared to project her voice. Stripped of her dysphoric guard uniform, she wore the epitome of empowerment, a borrowed leather jacket that reflected the fire in a brilliant light.

"Good evening, everyone. I think most of you know who I am, but for those who don't, I'm Juneau. First and foremost, I want to say thank you all for being here, for trusting me, for your sacrifices, and for your willingness to fight back against those who wish to constrain our freedom of expression. You have my sincerest gratitude. I know I speak for our whole group when I say that we are forever in your debt. You are, without a doubt, the strongest group of individuals I've ever had the honor to know.

"Now that you've had ample time to rest, I want to start planning for the future, and it must be a collective effort. What should our next steps be? Where do we go from here? Where do *you* want to go? Is the consensus to return to Springfield? Surely there will be repercussions from our escape, but keeping that in mind, we want to explore the next steps that are best for our community as a whole and for the personal well-being of each of you. The last thing I want to do is monopolize our next actions, but I want to fight back. All we've worked for, breaking you out of the Northeast Panoptic, it was all to get us here. So, you tell me."

Kieran patted Alex's shoulder and stood up, too. "Hell, yes! I want to put up a fight. Let's use this momentum to deal a one-two blow to the FPNG and their Panoptica. We need to keep fighting. We've accomplished a grand feat – something I would have deemed impossible – but while we have the fire in our bellies, why not keep fighting? The fight for acceptance and equality is far from over!" Kieran turned to gauge the general consensus: a whistle of approval from Jamie and a few cheers, lots of nodding. "All we need is an action plan."

Logan finally coughed and spoke up. "I'm not sure if this will be a popular opinion, but hear me out." Alex had noticed that Logan rarely spoke in large groups of people, so they sat up a bit straighter and focused their attention on them. Whatever it was that Logan was about to say, Alex presumed it was important.

"What happens if we choose not to go back? If we choose to defect from Springfield and wider society and maintain our isolation? To build a life of happiness and mutual validation here, or somewhere like here? I'm not sure about where semi-open nonbinary and gender nonconforming folks are safe these days, what kind of hidden communities may exist. We might not be validated or protected in the eyes of the Foundation or the systems in which they have their claws, but we sure as hell can protect one another. There's inherent value in prizing our safety. I'm don't know how many folks here share my opinion, but I'd rather not go back to the city, to Springfield, to more systematic suppression."

Juneau said, "Rather not return to fight for those we left behind, for those still stuck in those cities and towns, still locked in the Panoptica? Or for yourself?"

Logan's gaze was unwavering, unlike the crackling of the fire reflected in their eyes, lifting at the slightest hint of wind as if retreating from foreign echoes and whispers in the forest. "Yes, if it means safeguarding my livelihood. I don't want to fight every day until I die or am captured."

"Is it really better to abandon society than to improve it or fight for intuitional and social change when necessary?" Alex asked.

"Necessary is a relative term, Alex," Logan answered.

"That concept seems to be at the very core of the question Logan is asking," Xavier answered, dodging the heart of Alex's question. "Do we even have the resources to sustain everyone living here long-term?" He looked to Shay in particular for an answer.

"As of right now, with this many of people, we do not," she answered truthfully.

"Not even if we left camp and huddled down in safehouses in the area until we get established on our own terms?" Logan persisted.

"I doubt it," Shay repeated. "As I said to Alex earlier, there *are* folks who live here year-round in safehouses and those who run them, and they would be able to accommodate us in the meantime. But for long-term shelter? We'd be crowding them. And with the remote White Mountain Valley economy, I doubt everyone would be able to find suitable jobs, never mind make a comfortable living. Plus, I think the general consensus is that most people want to go back. Right?"

Alex agreed. "That's true. I miss my home, my family, Ryan. I sure don't want to be on the run forever, however tempting abandoning our pasts might seem at first."

"Plus," Juneau added, "the FPNG *will* come investigate the breakout. You can be sure of that. That puts our semi-remote camp and anyone still here at risk for discovery. Moreover, what was the point of everything we just did if not to spark a real change in this veritable hellscape?"

"There's something to be said for self-preservation," replied Logan.

"There's also something to be said for fighting for those who can't fight for or defend themselves."

Alex dropped a bomb into the already heated conversation. "Plus, in order to change society in the ways we want, we have to return to our homes, wherever they are. If the Foundation has taught me anything, it's that very few people are willing to fight on our behalf to disband the organization. But if most of us return, the enormous impact of us as an out, visible, tangible, nonbinary and gender nonconforming group cannot be understated. We'd be a living, physical representation of what it means to not only survive, but thrive."

Logan shrunk back down with the weight of Alex and Juneau's protestations, but before they could sit entirely, Alex extended a hand and gently guided them back up. "There's no shame in feeling how you do, Logan. I get it. Just because I want to fight back and return to Springfield doesn't mean that, deep down, I don't wish I could just peace out forever. I understand."

"I'm not a coward," Logan replied with firm instance.

"We know." Shay offered her support, too. "Would you be willing to hear me out, though? For what I have to offer?"

Logan relented, "Yes, of course."

Juneau stepped down to allow Shay access to the log-cum-dais. "Tell them your plan. I think they'll like what you have to say," Alex murmured in Shay's ear as she ascended, offering her a hand up.

"Here's what I propose," Shay began, once again assuming her role as natural leader. "My Gran has a place nearby, in Bartlett. A sizeable farm, farmhouse, outbuildings. We can't survive much longer at camp here. The snow has definitely set in for the season, and it's encroaching on our ability to subsist in tents much longer."

"Definitely. We've probably stretched the season a bit far as it is," Jamie confirmed.

"So," Shay continued, "I propose that we head over to Gran's place immediately. Break up into small groups for the journey to make our party less conspicuous. Some of y'all know about other safehouses in the area, so please reach out to your contacts; Gran won't be able to fit all of us. A group of our size will be noticed, and who knows what would happen if we were detected. I don't want to risk anyone's safety at this point, and I'm certain you all don't either. What do you say?"

Xavier raised his hand, and the crowd parted to give him room to push to the front of the throng. "And then what?"

"Then, we launch an offensive," Shay said.

"How?"

"Good question."

"Definitely," Alex perked up. "Fair question. We do need to start thinking further ahead. But also, I say we get everyone out of here and rendezvous at Shay's Gran's house safely, and once we're there, we can make some serious plans."

Kieran stepped up. "As long as we formulate something definitive, a real strategy, I'm game."

"Will you come with us, Logan? To Shay's Gran's house? Whether you choose to return to Springfield or not, we'd want you there," Alex insisted.

"Yes, I will join you," they agreed.

"Jumping off of that," Shay announced, "I have conferred with Juneau, Jamie, and some of the others, and we should probably have a head council of sorts, a core team to direct everyone. What are your thoughts? Any concerns?"

A chorus of insistent head nods followed, and someone asked, "Can anyone join?"

"Absolutely." Shay looked around at the faces filled with fervor, but when no one else spoke up, she took it as silent approval. "Okay then. Depending on how plentiful our rations are, this might be our last night here. So for now, just relax and rest up. We'll come together for dinner in an hour. Thanks, everyone."

Everyone filtered away, back to their smaller groups, some into tents and some sat around other fires. Alex wanted nothing more than relaxation and private time with Kieran, but they sensed they should remain at the fire, that something more needed to be said. Sure enough, Juneau and Shay approached Alex, and they braced for impact.

"Alex, we want you to join our council. As makeshift as it is for now, an ersatz version of what it could be for our movement in the future, we need you." Shay's tone informed Alex that she was more than resolute in her decision, but Alex still felt they were unfit for the role. They steadfastly expressed their hesitance.

"Alex, why are you doubting yourself?"

"I've never seen myself as a leader. Why me?" That had been Alex's consistent mantra at every stage of their escape. *But,* they wondered, *aren't the answers right before my eyes? I risked my personal safety for Juneau's sake. I assisted in the conquer of the guard tower because she insisted; she needed people she trusted, and I stepped up. I've proven my worth in regards to performing under stress. I guess I shouldn't be all that surprised.*

Why don't I recognize these traits – assurance, confidence, sacrifice – in myself?

"You may not yet think this of yourself," Juneau said, "But you've grown immensely since I left for the Northeast Panoptic, Alex. This experience has evolved you. Even just now, you were outspoken and determined to fight for your own rights and for the sake of others' liberation from systematic oppression. You may still be scared, but I can see confidence brewing in you. It's evident to those around you. You spoke up tonight, many times. We need your steady voice and your courage."

"I *am* scared."

Shay nodded. "As are we. But with your energy, especially your creative energy, we know you can do this. I'm sure Ryan would agree with me."

"Most definitely," Juneau concurred. "As I told you back in the Panoptic, we need people we can trust."

"I still see myself as weak and paralyzed with inaction. It's hard to mentally crack that shell and see myself any other way."

Shay practically chortled. "Please, you're not meek. Far from it. To survive under the oppression and pressure you faced every day, Alex, that requires incredible strength. You still have that strength today. You're stronger than you think."

The stark, bold font of those well-advertised and well-circulated Foundation for the Protection of Normative Gender flyers – those defined, binarized gender definitions and presentations – flitted across Alex's mind. *Biological Sex. Male. Female. Major Hormonal Makeup. Estrogen. Testosterone. Required. Required Genitals. Allowed. Not Allowed. Strictly Prohibited.* "Well, yeah, but…"

"But nothing. You are a strong person, full stop. You've struggled, I've seen it," Juneau admitted. "To help decide what we do next, to be that agent of change if you want to be, that's just as much your right as anyone else's. Remember what I told you in the Panoptic?"

Alex grumbled a long string of incoherent words and several expletives, so low that not even Kieran, who was right at Alex's shoulder, could hear them. Juneau had a point, and Alex disliked it. They *did* have just as much right as anyone to have a hand in altering the status quo. They had important opinions; they wanted to do something to change society. Still, they harbored an internalized fear of the repercussions of speaking up and speaking out, and fear of being on the firing line for doing so. *But who better than me to follow through?* they thought, not for the first time.

Who better than Alex to do it? To put all those so-called "revolutionary thoughts" into action, to see them through to fruition? To water and nourish the seeds of change?

"Okay," they said, nearly silently.

"Huh?" both Juneau and Shay asked.

"OKAY," Alex repeated, louder and sterner. "Okay, you're right. I'll join. You've seen something in me, and I desperately want to see it for myself, to exert that confidence and determination you insist I possess."

"YES!!" Alex knew Juneau to be a fairly serious and stoic person in times like these, but she literally jumped for joy and slapped Alex's hand in a high five that made Alex laugh harder than they had in a while.

"Yes, yes, y'all convinced me. Now what?"

***

Thus began Alex's third exodus of the season: first from Springfield to Mount Washington's summit, then from the summit to the base camp, and now, from camp to Bartlett for Shay's Gran's place.

By car, the trip would have taken maybe an hour and a half, given the weather and the seasonal tourist traffic. For experienced hikers? The journey would be about seven hours. But by foot and considering the size of their group, their weakening wills, fatigue, and hungry bellies, it took two days before they finally arrived on the outskirts of Bartlett, just ten minutes or so from her Gran's house, Shay promised. Opting to avoid any and all main roads, they chose the harsher, more treacherous route of trekking down the mountain, through Crawford Notch State Park, into the part of Bartlett that borders on Hart's Location, versus the alternative of walking along the former Mount Washington Auto Road. Not many people would be eager to chance this descent after the most recent storm, no matter how good their four-wheel drive was.

Three things invigorated Alex during this brutal trek: the sweet, pure, pine-scented air that smelled of Christmas morning; Kieran's hand in theirs; and hope. Weighing them down, however, were the blisters mounting on the edges of Alex's feet due to their uncomfortable boots, a deep chill that they couldn't shake no matter how closely they cuddled with Kieran at night, and several days' long hunger. They longed for a warm, full belly, to be sustained rather than run down. For Alex, these two days of travel were a cold, bitter purgatory. *In the movies, after the heroes accomplish their mammoth, supposedly final task, they gain immediate celebration, recognition, praise, and redemption.* But this journey was more drudgery, more difficulty, and seemingly endless suffering.

When will we get that recognition? they wondered. *Maybe that means we're not at the end?* Then Alex reminded themselves, *Of course we're not at the end. There's work yet to be done.*

It may not have been a warm meal or toasty shoes, but the hearty sight of Shay's Gran's nineteenth century colonial home, smoke puttering out in puffs from the chimney, brought Alex some measure of joy and even a little rejuvenation. The sloping, mopey hills in the vicinity hugged the expansive farm property, the main feature of which was Gran's house itself: a midnight-blue, sprawling colonial farmhouse, which looked to Alex like something out of the movie *The Crucible* or a fixture fit for Salem, Massachusetts. Even from this far away, Alex spotted the bright red door, akin to the flashing bulb of a lighthouse, both calling them to comfort and warning them of the nearby rocky coast.

"We're home, kids," Shay announced from the back of the group as they panted their way to the top of the last hill separating them from Gran's homestead.

CHAPTER 21

A steady melody of *clinks*, *clangs*, scraping knives, the *dings* of toasting glasses and hollers echoed in an arhythmic cacophony down the length of Gran's long farm tables shoved together, which spanned the living rooms, kitchen, and dining rooms so there was room for all, everyone shoulder to shoulder with their comrades.

After hours, days, and years surviving without total peace and comfort, Alex, for the first time in a while, felt full: full of substantial food, full of hope, full of relative happiness, and full of acceptance. Alex had zero clue how Shay's Gran conjured this bountiful smorgasbord to feed fifty people, but it felt like a miracle. Gran's old farmhouse colonial itself was a thing of hybrid beauty. It retained its nineteenth century charm with original hardwood floors and thick, rustic beams running straight across the ceiling in every room, but it had also been expanded and renovated over the years. The house contained several wide-open community spaces: the living rooms, the dining room, the wraparound porch, and back deck. But for containing so many inviting meeting places, Gran's house also held many hiding holes: bedrooms and lofts, some grand like the master bedroom with a near-panoramic view of the mountains, and some cozy, only wide enough to fit two double bunks like an undergraduate dorm room. While Kieran was napping before dinner, Alex wandered every inch of the place; they loved mapping out spaces.

Gran herself was an absolute marvel. Not only had she opened her life and her home to Alex and their bunch, literal fugitives (and so many of them!), but most memorably, she had asked each and every person's name and pronouns upon arrival, introducing herself in the same manner.

Although her five foot, two inch stature was small, the glint in her gray eyes was formidable and fierce. She was a woman to be awed and respected, and she reminded Alex of Shay in that way. *Must be where Shay got her fortitude from.*

But Xavier dropped an anvil into the disarming comfort of dinner; after gulping down a bit of lightly salted roasted potatoes, he raised his voice barely over the residual clanking to address anyone who could hear him, but Juneau was his intended audience. "Guys, we're kind of a disorganized mess."

Juneau didn't hear him at first. She was too busy telling Logan where Jamie was: "They're at another safehouse with some others from camp. We wanted to distribute as many leaders to other groups as possible." Noting that she was currently embroiled in another conversation, Gran leaned toward Xavier and asked, "Why do you think that, uh…"

"Xavier, ma'am."

"Please, call me Gran. You're family now."

Xavier smiled briefly, but his face quickly fell. "It seems too obvious to state, but we barely know who is where and with whom and how many people escaped. We freed hundreds of people, I'd wager. Where are they all? Did they all get to some manner of safety? How many were recaptured? We already had to split up our core group into a few other safehouses, but the rest…"

Juneau overheard and elbowed her way back in. "Xavier, I was just speaking with Logan and told them that Jamie is just down the road. We do have central leaders in place to make cross-house communication a bit easier so we can unite the front." She offered a small smile, hoping it would offer some form of comfort and prompt Xavier to let the issue lie for now.

Not to be deterred, Xavier said, "Do people have room for them? I can only imagine that hundreds of folks are seeking shelter in this area."

"We'll make do."

Gran leapt in to defuse the tension. "The rest will be fine, and will come in time. You all need time to plan, to take stock, to fill your bellies, to nourish your bodies, and to regroup. No matter how determined, passionate, and well-intentioned, every strong, important movement begins with a little disorganization, a little chaos. It's par for the course in human matters."

"But…"

"You all will mature and foster it. Fear not."

A moment passed in which most everyone trained their eyes back onto their plates and picked at the remaining morsels left there. But Alex's head remained up. The wisdom of Gran's words had Alex intrigued. "I'd like to hear more about you, Gran. Where did you grow up? What was it like? How and why did you settle down out here?"

Taking her seat again and consuming her last piece of broccoli, Gran reveled in the spotlight. "Certainly! I'm always eager to tell a story."

"That's for sure," Shay chuckled. "Gran likes to talk. Not that that's a bad thing!"

"Oh, you hush now," Gran said as she feigned to shoo her granddaughter away. "You want to know more about me, huh? Well, like many of you, I grew up in the city. Springfield, in fact. Springfield is tricky. Although it's a major city, it's small enough that the Foundation can closely monitor more people than, say, New York City."

Her guests nodded, especially Alex. *Good point*, they agreed. Despite its growing population, the Foundation kept annoyingly close tabs on the citizens, ready to sniff out any variance in their midst.

Gran continued, "You'll find, surprisingly, that it's hard to police gender in those major metropoles, like New York, though perhaps not as hard as the farther flung reaches, as with us here."

"I was surprised when you told me that you used to live near the city, Gran. You hate big crowds of people," Shay said.

Gran dished her a coy wink. "That's why I left to live in the middle of the mountains as soon as I had the choice and the means, my dear."

Alex asked, "And you don't mind taking us all in while we're here?"

"Not in the least. If I can save even a few people, especially youngsters like you, that's more important than my isolated privacy. As a kid, I loved the mountains. I adored the sublimity of it all, of how different this region is compared to those others around us. I still do. Have you ever hiked up to Cathedral's Ledge? Or taken a stroll along Diana's Baths here in Bartlett, or a hike up to Arethusa Falls in Crawford Notch? I remember this one time…"

"I think they get it, Gran," Shay urged with an exhausted tone. "Maybe stay on track for this one."

Gran laughed Shay off, as one does a child when they ask something so obviously silly. "Backtracking to add all those details for context is important, hon. I've found that the more background details you can learn about a person, the more context you have to see how and why someone is the way they are. Whether it's their upbringing or experiences, with more color and context, you start to get to the core of who someone is and who they've become.

"Anywho. It still disappoints me to say this, but my parents were not nearly as supportive of me as I am of Shay or any of y'all. It's still hard to relive, all these years later. I told my parents I was agender on holiday break in fifth grade..."

Alex felt the theoretical mic drop in their head. Gran was agender too? Then again, the announcement shouldn't have shocked them because who were they to presume who Gran was? They hadn't asked her, after all.

"... and they weren't receptive in the least. Middle school was torturous. Does anyone like middle school? There I was in the horrid throes of puberty – menstruation, the whole nine yards – and my parents made it more difficult, more insufferable. Their scrutiny was worse than even the 'normal' teasing of my peers since I was a bit chubby.

"I fought back, I spoke out, I rebelled, and I resisted my parents at every turn. I can't imagine it was easy for them to sell out their own child, but who cares now." Gran offered a noncommittal shrug.

"They sold you out?!" Alex was aghast. Their stomach hardened, and the pit of anxiety housed there swelled at hearing those words.

Gran offered a long sigh, finally put down her fork, and said, "Yes. Freshman year of high school. I was shipped off here, if you can believe it. I think they actually thought that the regimen of strict gender structure and reeducation classes would be 'good for me.'"

"To Bartlett?" Xavier asked, but Shay shook her head and corrected him.

"The Panoptic."

"Holy shit."

"Imprisonment was another horrid piece of punctuation in my already depressing life. I was kicked further into a pit of depression that I still struggle to resolve. Even today, I am working to process my feelings from long ago. I lost my best friend Tim in there."

"How? Dare I ask?" Xavier proceeded.

"Unfortunately, he took his own life."

The entire table was silent as a grave, in acknowledgment of Gran's loss. Not a scrape or clatter was heard, and they all waited respectfully for her to resume her history when she was ready. In time, she said, "I swore that after Tim, I would do everything in my power to help young folks just like yourselves and like my Shay, one day aspiring to set up a safehouse in the area. So, I played my cards right, acted my part to 'conform,' and six months later, they sent me home. Upon my return, I spent one last night in Springfield, gathering my things while my parents were out with friends. I was only fifteen years old, but already having to find my own way in the world because of bigotry and hate.

"Thanks to the graciousness of friends with licenses and cars, I trekked up to the Bartlett area and couch-surfed for a time until I got a few local jobs, met some nice, older, nonbinary and gender nonconforming folks.

"Eventually, I was privileged enough to settle down in this here house permanently with…"

"Hey hon, I'm home!" The call came from the back door in the kitchen, and in swept a gorgeous person in a heavy wool, princess cut peacoat, knocking their snow-caked boots off on the designated floor mat and shrugging off all their outerwear.

"My wife, Abby," Gran presented. "She's a doctor at the White Mountains regional hospital."

Abby kissed Gran hello, drew herself up a chair, cobbled together bits of leftover food from the feast, and settled in to introduce herself to the group.

CHAPTER 22

"Alex, holy crepes, is that you?!" Alex had never heard Ryan's voice so high-pitched as they held the mobile phone they'd borrowed from Gran away from their head to keep from going deaf in one ear from his excitement. They were on their second and last call home of the day: first Jo, then Ryan.

Alex had to laugh at the incredulity of it all: here they were on the phone with Ryan, much like any other night, except in this instance, they could claim the status of newly escaped prisoner, a fugitive from the law and the FPNG. They never imagined that this would be their life.

A gust of wind roared against the side of Gran's house, rattling a few of the older windows in their slanted panes and brushing static across the phone line, causing Alex to miss whatever Ryan said next. With many of the trees as bare as they were in Bartlett, the wind howled with strong force against the old colonial, followed by the gentle patter of rain tapping at the front door.

Alex lost themselves in the addictive sound. *If there's no snow tonight, we should expect fog tomorrow, from the warming rain mixing with hard-packed snow.*

"Huh? What did you say? Sorry, Ryan, the wind's kicking up in the mountains."

"The mountains? Where are you? How did you get access to a phone? I thought they arrested you. Tell me everything!"

"Ryan, cool it!"

"No. No, Alex, I need to know you're safe."

"I am."

"Where, damn it?"

Alex drew in a long breath and exhaled a sigh just as lengthy. "You won't believe me when I tell you this, but I'm actually staying with…"

The ellipses of silence that followed as Alex trailed off unseated Ryan, and he fired off his next question with little hesitation. "What?"

"Ryan, where are you?"

"At home."

"On your phone?"

Alex knew Ryan so well that they could sense him smiling on the other end of the line, smiling at Alex's paranoia. They couldn't explain it, they just knew. Best friend intuition, perhaps. *Why would he be smiling at a time like this?* Alex focused on determining how much information they should really divulge over the phone.

"A prepaid phone, actually. My old one's getting fixed. I dropped it on the pavement, dumbass me." Alex figured it was probably safe to resume their narrative. This was Ryan, after all.

So, they continued with great caution. "I'm with Shay's Gran right now, actually."

"No way!"

Alex couldn't wait for Ryan to finish his exclamation, so they forged onward. "It gets better. Guess who else I'm with?"

"Haha, who else now?"

"Juneau."

There was radio silence on Ryan's end of the phone, and Alex pictured him gulping like a freshly caught sea bass, floundering for the proper response, fishing for the exact words to say. "Did… did I hear you right?" Ryan asked. "You said that… that you're with Juneau?" The full weight of his adoration and longing were apparent in how he settled on her name with emphasis, like he didn't want to let go of her name.

Alex wanted nothing more than to reach through the line and grip him in a solid hug. "You heard right, Ryan. And she's doing really well."

"How's… how's she doing?" His question was timid, as if he was afraid of the answer, afraid to hear the horrible things she must have endured.

"Ryan, I just said that! She's fine! We're all mostly fine."

"Where has she been?" He paused, forgetting himself and forgetting the reason for Alex's call in the first place. "Where have *you* been? I miss you and I need you here."

"I miss you, too, you know that. It's honestly a super long story. You ready?"

"Yes, dish it to me." His insistence was crisp and betrayed little hesitation.

And so, Alex did. It took over an hour of nonstop talking to relay their journey, thousands of words illustrating the experience in the most detail they could manage. Alex loved having Ryan at their side, seeing him almost every day. To feel that sense of closeness again, that sense of intimate friendship, to reconnect with him, they needed him to know every single thing about the last month, since he hadn't been there himself. And when Alex's recount caught them up to present day, Ryan rattled off the last words Alex wanted to hear, and the very words that everyone kept asking both them and each other.

"So, now what?"

***

"So, now what?" Alex had to physically restrain themselves from rolling their eyes as Kieran asked Alex that very same question the following morning, on day two of their stay in Gran's abode. How was Kieran to know that Ryan had annoyed them the night before with the very same question? They tried unsuccessfully to drown out Kieran's question by humming "Winter Wonderland" as forcefully and cheerily as they could, as the couple trudged through the mucky snow and the remainder of last night's incessant rainfall.

They had borrowed a couple of pairs of old wellies from Gran so they could go for a walk on the circular paths that wound around the hill closest to her house. Privacy was what they both craved, which was definitely a rarity in their current situation. Aside from their nights camping in the tent, the last moment they spent alone was in their private-ish reuniting moment, the roiling chaos of the overthrow of the Panoptic when Alex spotted Kieran in the atrium.

Trade the lavender-hued blue jays and deep scarlet cardinals for copper and cerulean bluebirds, and the jaunt was cut from the same cloth as the music sheet on which the song "Winter Wonderland" was written.

Only I definitely don't want to get married while I'm in town, Alex thought.

Drawing themselves up to fully process Kieran's question, Alex stopped in their tracks, sighed, and disconnected from Kieran's hand as they brought theirs to their temple to rub out the tendrils of the headache that was slowly creeping in.

"I don't know, all right! I don't know."

"You must know something," Kieran countered, "being as close with the powers that be as you are."

"Powers that be?"

Kieran shrugged. "You know, Juneau and the others. The leaders? The council? The one you're a part of?"

"You mean the one *you* could join, too? I'm not a conduit or messenger, Kieran."

"So, here's the sixty-four-thousand-dollar question: what's the plan?"

Alex actually rolled their eyes at this remark. Rarely did Alex put their hands on their hips and *harrumph*, but if any situation called for it, it was this one. "Kieran, do you seriously think I'm keeping something from you? Whatever I know, you know. Do you think I'm going to betray you or shelter you or something?"

"No, of course not, but…"

"But what?"

"I hate not knowing, okay!" Kieran snapped and threw their hands up into fists. "Vague plans and promises, the middle grounds, neither here nor there, the indecision. I hate it. Uncertainty is my absolute enemy."

Alex's response was hesitant, tender. "You and I are much alike in that way. Are you sure this isn't actually about something else, Kieran?"

"You're dang right, it is."

"Well, then," pushed Alex, prickling up like a disgruntled porcupine, "spit it out. What's wrong?"

"Oh my gods, Alex, are you really still *this* thick?" Alex guessed at what Kieran was saying, but just because they thought they knew, didn't mean they wanted to deprive themselves of hearing the actual words. If Kieran said what they expected, it would make the situation more real, more remarkable, than if Alex had stolen those words from them. Alex *wanted* Kieran to say them, *wanted* that external, obvious recognition of affection and commitment, though they were equally scared of both. For Alex, who overthought almost every situation in their lives, that verbal recognition of someone's feelings or intentions was critical.

"I like you. A lot," Kieran started. "You know that, I know that. I want to be with you, Alex, for you to be my partner, girlfriend, boyfriend, date-mate, whatever you want to be called. I want to be with you more than anything. Like *for real* be with you."

Alex couldn't keep the smile from subtly slinking up their lips. "Even more than…"

"Yes." Kieran couldn't let them finish. "Even more than the cause. Please. Please tell me you feel the same way."

"You *are* with me, but…"

"But what?"

The constant interjections annoyed Alex, but they obliged. Kieran looked desperate, as desperate as Alex was to kiss them in that very moment. "I want to focus on the tasks at hand before I focus more attention on our relationship. If we have the slight chance of succeeding with this goal of ours, surviving even, we have to give it everything. I don't want to promise you anything with both of our futures still so unknown. Please, can you understand?"

"So," Kieran said. "After this is over…"

"After we return to the city and do what we need to do, all of my attention goes to us. It's not that I don't want to go all in. I want that more than…"

"More than what?"

"More than almost anything."

"Okay," Kieran relented.

Alex grabbed them in a full-bodied hug and whispered, "I love you."

"I love you, too," was Kieran's soft but insistent reply.

CHAPTER 23

"All right everyone," Shay began, clapping her hands together to open the meeting she'd called in Gran's barn the following evening. Lanterns hung in rustic sconces along the barn's three main walls, and the ten-foot-tall, ruby-red doors sat six inches ajar, so she could keep an eye on anyone entering the vicinity, friend or intruder.

Especially for this 4:30 p.m. dusk, the barn was bitterly cold. Each member of the gathering huffed out dragon-like plumes of steam like a multifaceted fog machine, something of the steampunk era, perhaps. The faint smell of snow danced through the air. And though the barn was frigid, it was one of the few structures in the area capable of housing almost every Northeast Panoptic refugee for the brief meeting. The rest of the folks, still stashed away in safehouses, would have to settle for hearing the results of this gathering second-hand.

"I want to hear your ideas for how we can return to Springfield, and what to do once we've arrived, if that's still the plan. We're open to any suggestions. One at a time, please."

Like that is going to happen, Alex scoffed, and a rising roar of voices erupted on the cusp of Shay's last word.

"Where are we going?"

"Springfield, she said. You heard her."

"Why? Why go at all?"

"It's the closest major city."

"What about Manchester? Portsmouth? Portland? Aren't those major cities?"

"But the Foundation, the FPNG, that's our target. They have their major headquarters in Springfield."

"Yeah! Everyone will be convening there when they hear our plan if we circulate our action items coherently and covertly. We should, too."

"But surely they'll cover this up, right?"

"How could they possibly cover up something on this scale?"

"Guys, guys! Folks! People!" Shay waved her hands in wild circles but everyone ignored her and broke out by the dozens into their own conversations, voicing their ideas, assumptions, speculations, and desires. The rushing tide of voices drowned her out completely, and Alex floundered helplessly in the crowd; they didn't feel their voice was strong enough to break through.

"Springfield, huh?"

"So how do we get there?"

"Buses, trains?"

"All of us? Too conspicuous."

"What if we walk?"

"A caravan of fugitives? Right, *that's* not conspicuous, either…"

"Well, what do you suggest?"

"Take a bunch of cars? Split ourselves up?"

"Split ourselves up?!"

Beneath all these explanations, exclamations, proposals, and questions was a consistent undercurrent of quieter voices. "Why not stay here?" and "Should we even go back?" and "We're safer here, right?"

"My Gran knows someone with a bus," Shay loudly told Alex over the roaring cacophony of voices and conflicting opinions.

"Wait, for real?" Alex replied. "Where did they get one of those?"

"Gran knows…" Shay began, but the rest was lost in the din.

"Come again?" they asked.

Shay scooted over and moved Kieran out of the way to speak directly into Alex's ear. "Gran's friend is a school bus driver in the area."

"That won't take care of all of us."

"I know! I have a backup plan, too. I think I heard someone shout something similar to what I was thinking. If I could only get everyone to…"

A deafening whistle originated from Gran's lips outside the barn doors and pierced through the commotion, quieting the roaring conversations in an instant.

"Thanks, Gran," Shay laughed, and she dove into her plan to get the enthusiastic group back home.

***

Together, Alex, Shay, Kieran, Juneau, Xavier, Logan, Jamie, and all those who gathered that night stitched together a plan – *the* plan – threading and knotting any loose threads as tightly as they could manage from the resources at their disposal. Like a reverse Pangea, they began to suture together critical details from several ideas, until they'd creating an executable plan, working diligently and precisely so that the dominoes all fell in their intended places. Care was required to tip the scales in their favor for those folks on the fence of participation, some hoping that this plan was more than an illusion or pipe dream.

Could this work? Would this work? Alex thought as they were mid-negotiation. Doubts crept into the cracks, nudging their way into Alex's mind, born from uncertainties and the unknown variables for which they could not hope to plan.

A vote cast toward the end of the meeting raised far more yays than nays, and with that confirmation, they were off; the starting gun crackled to life and the race was on to lay the foundation for the next stage of their scheme.

A few folks resolutely decided to stay behind with Gran. Alex was unsurprised to see Logan among this group, but they didn't resent Logan for their decision. Instead, Alex left the meeting with a hug and a handshake for them, remarking, "We *will* meet again."

Logan had nodded in reply.

That night, Alex insisted on carving out time alone with their thoughts before squeezing into bed with Kieran: time to recall, to revisit, to reflect, and to write. They borrowed a notebook – Gran had plenty to spare – and plopped down on her rough wooden deck for twenty minutes. They scribbled, crossed out, and then scribbled some more, refining their thoughts. Finally, they were satisfied with their piece:

> *They say the world will end in either fire*
> *or in ice*

But when the Second Coming's nascent,
sleet-laced droplets
Sound the same as a crackling hearth fire in the half-
awake dawn.
I ask:
"What's the difference?"

Ice is forged from fire.

CHAPTER 24

And so, they flocked like geese soaring south for the winter; like the queen marching ahead to check an opposing king on a chessboard so weathered that the varnish is faded and flaking; like Icarus' ascent into the sun, they flew from all angles: from up in Maine to the White Mountains, from southeastern Vermont to Connecticut, and even a round of folks from the southernmost tip of New Brunswick, friends, family, allies, and even gender nonconforming and nonbinary people themselves flocked to the epicenter of Springfield.

Alex was merely one fish converging in a sea of thousands.

They rode shotgun in a crammed car alongside Kieran, who was driving, Juneau, Jamie, Xavier, and two new friends into the city. Many others from Bartlett were making that same journey in borrowed cars and cars of their own. Heck, even a school bus was part of the caravan. But to outsiders, to strangers zooming along in their own cars, buses, trucks, and other vehicles on the highway, nothing was amiss. Here was Alex, a member of a secret fleet paving their purpose in broad daylight, and no one was the wiser.

Or so they hoped, briefly recalling Officer Paine's persistence back at the Panoptic.

"Where should we meet?" Ryan had asked Alex earlier that morning on a last call before they hit the road.

"Springfield City Hall. That's where everyone is converging."

"Not just those in-state, I assume?"

"Nope. From the group that escaped the Northeast Panoptic, most of us are coming, not to mention our fellows, colleagues, and supports within and from outside of the city. But the network, Ryan, our network is *huge*, to my surprise, really. All the people Jamie and Juneau know. It's unreal."

"How many? We talking hundreds?"

"Thousands, Ryan. Thousands."

"Dang…" Ryan had blown out a long sigh over the line, and while they didn't have much time left on the call, he had given Alex the impression that he wanted to cling to the conversation, a safety buffer before the action commenced. "Anything online about it?"

"Not yet. We're keeping it under wraps, well, until…"

"Until we all show up at City Hall, haha," Ryan had finished.

"Yup, exactly. Ryan, I have to go. Other folks need the line to call, just to call around. We're spreading the word verbally and we still have some folks we need to inform. Gotta gather the numbers, you know."

"Where are they from? I can't believe there are that many of us in the area, in the network."

"I know. They're coming from everywhere, honestly. All across New England, and there's rumored to be some people coming down from Canada for support. I gotta go. Bye, Ryan. See you soon."

"Wait!" Ryan exclaimed, catching Alex right before they hung up. "Why today?"

Alex chuckled. "Don't you know, Ryan? Today's the Foundation's birthday."

"Damn, you're right. Have fun with the call tree. See you soon. Love ya."

"Love ya, too."

***

On a train lugging itself into Springfield's North Station, just a mile from the city center and Springfield City Hall, a graying man asked a twenty-something college student if the poster board they held close was for a school project. The young student lied with a kind smile, "Yup! It's for a project I've been working on." For now, they kept their battle cry hidden:

Nonbinary Lives Matter.
Nonbinary Trans Lives Matter.

***

A middle school teen waved goodbye to their moms as they ran out to their friend's car idling in the driveway. One of their moms asked, "When will you be home? Give me a buzz on your way back."

"I'll only be out for a few hours, just going to the mall!"

"Okay, be safe!"

The teen hopped into the car and asked their friend driving, "Hey, you mind if I plug my phone in on the way? I wanna capture every moment of this."

***

A middle-aged, nonbinary, femme, trans woman just finished printing the last batch of letter-fold flyers from her computer, using vibrant yellow and purple streaks across their title page, calling for inclusive gender policy reform.

***

A man kissed his husband on the forehead and lips and, tucking an errant curl of strawberry blond hair behind his ear, insisted, "Call us when you get into the city, and stay safe."

"I will," the husband reaffirmed with a final peck of his own. He waved to his wriggling, giggling twin children in their highchairs as he swiped a jacket from the coatrack and closed the front door firmly behind him.

***

Logan inched closer to Gran's radio, dry, nervous fingers flipping between stations until Gran rested a gentle hand upon theirs and hummed, "Soon, it's nearly time. Take a deep breath, child."

Eyes glistening, fighting with their guilt, Logan asked her, "Should I feel bad for staying behind? What if they need me?"

"Logan, they need you happy and healthy. You're exactly where you're supposed to be."

***

Alex's mum absently bit at the fingernails on her right hand, her left holding her husband's hand. With sleepless eyes, they mindlessly watched the local news channel, waiting for time to pass.

***

Ryan tore himself away from his parents as they begged him to let them know where he was going. "I'm just going to study with a few friends," he lied, slinging his backpack across his left shoulder on the way out, ignoring their concerned expressions. "I promise."

"Just be careful," Ryan's dad pleaded. "You remember what happened to…"

Ryan shot his dad a death glare and said, "Don't. I know what's coming next. I will never forget what happened to Alex. Besides, I have a good feeling they'll be back in no time." He firmly closed the front door on his way out.

***

Back in their borrowed car two hours later, Alex double-, triple-, and quadruple-checked with Xavier until he promised this should work.

"You'd think we could do better than *should*!"

"That's the best I got, Alex."

"All right." They turned back to face the front windshield; it was a perfectly clear day by all respects. Moments later, they hit the Springfield turnpike and enjoyed the brief respite of free-flowing traffic before they hit the expected congestion closer to the city's border as the maze of twisting highways converged. Springfield's landmark white concrete suspension bridge soon peeked its way into their sightline, and the realization that they were close sent nervous ripples through Alex's stomach.

Kieran nudged Alex. "You'd better call Ryan."

"All right."

***

"Ryan?"

"Yeah? What's up, Alex? I can barely hear you," he shouted over the clamor. In the background, Alex detected scuffling and the disjointed ends and beginnings of random conversations. A few shouts here and there, honking horns and digital walkways commanding "Wait! Wait!" until the cars given the green light passed and the intersections safely opened up for pedestrians.

Alex clicked the volume on their burner cell phone up a few notches, not that it was going to help much, but it gave them the illusion that they could hear Ryan better. "Wow, you're down there already?"

"Will be soon. What's up?"

"So, uh…"

Alex's sentence drifting off, resulting in Ryan yelling, "Huh?"

"We just hit the turnpike and the Springfield Suspension Bridge is in view. Before I meet you at City Hall, there's something I'm doing first."

"Better not be dangerous."

"Nope, I'm good. Just tell as many folks as you can to tweet up a storm while you're waiting for me, like we agreed upon."

"You got it, Alex."

Juneau shouted from the back of the car, "As many banned words as you can muster, Ryan!"

"You got it," Ryan replied vaguely. "Wait, was that… was that you, Alex?"

"Nope, that was Juneau."

Ryan's voice faded into silence as the background noises of downtown Springfield drowned him out. "Hey there," he finally recovered. "I'll see y'all soon. Be safe. How will I know when you're done with whatever task you're about to undertake?"

"You'll know," they replied.

"It better not be dangerous," he warned.

"Oh no, nothing like that. Don't worry, Ryan. I promise I will be safe." At that, they pressed the End Call button.

"Hey, Alex." Xavier poked them on the shoulder from the back seat. "Better get started, huh?"

"Yep. We're coming up on the city."

"I made an anonymous account. You want to tweet from that, too?"

"No thanks, Xavier. I'll use my own. I think I should," Alex confirmed.

CHAPTER 25

The energy in the city had changed since the last time they were amidst these skyscrapers; it was as palpable as the beating sun on Alex's face and the wind whipping in such a way that it snatched the beanie right off their head. They drove by scores of people on their way to the Government Center parking garage. Neither Alex nor Kieran, Xavier, or Juneau could discern if these were simply people going about their daily business or if they were flocking to City Hall for the protests. Alex thought they saw people speckled here and there with signs in their hands, but they couldn't be sure as Kieran drove them straight into the darkness of the parking garage, obscuring their sight.

After parking their car and jogging down three flights of gloomy, concrete stairs, the group kept their heads down as they waded through the crowds to State Street, taking a hard left at the double crosswalk intersection that connected the sprawling market shops with City Hall. Up three more streets sat the University of Springfield's School of Communications building, where Jamie's friend Mattie led them up to the university's student-led radio studio.

"I bet you've never broadcasted anything like this, eh, Mattie?" Juneau asked.

Mattie laughed and swept their long, black, straightened hair out of their face. "Nope, nothing of the sort. You've got your people ready?"

"They know what time we're broadcasting," Juneau confirmed. She checked her watch. "Speaking of which, it's nearly two o'clock. You ready, Alex?"

Alex gulped down their nervousness, and despite the slight shake to their hands, they replied with conviction. "Yes, I'm ready. Set me up."

***

Ryan knew – they all knew – what had to be done; there was a certain order of concrete events, but the gathering he helped organize, both online and in person, was crucial. To limit the possibility of exposure or tampering, only a few people knew that the University of Springfield's radio station was their main target, and all the rest would come in time. Like dominoes, each event would topple the next and so on and so on to catalyze the (hopefully) strong uproar on which Alex and company were banking.

To Ryan's pleasant shock, thousands of people were gathered at Springfield City Hall, and they were certainly getting questioning looks from the general public. He had also heard through the grapevine that Springfield's police force was on their way, perhaps because passersby saw the burgeoning gathering as a public safety issue; the masses had zero warning about a protest that day. Just as planned.

Meanwhile, a virtual onslaught was underway as the Twitterverse exploded with a fireworks display of thousands of tweets, and Ryan was sure their movement was on the cusp of going viral with their unifying hashtag, which Ryan himself was tweeting relentlessly:

#DownWithPanoptica

The rising tide of momentum was officially underway.

Ryan: Want to see the #FallofPanoptic? We've got evidence, so stay tuned. #DownWithPanoptica

Ryan could not refresh his feed fast enough to keep track of the new tweets, retweets, responses, and questions directed at folks on the hashtag. His singular focus was the same as many folks with him both physically and virtually: to push out a singular message that nonbinary and gender nonconforming folks had successfully conquered the Northeast Panoptic and were on the cusp of sharing that story with the public. He also retweeted several secondary hashtags:

#WeAreValid
#EnbiesAreValid
#WeAreVisible

#ValidateEnbiesNow
#DownWithFPNG
#SpringfieldProtest
#MoreThan4Genders

Ryan: Today's the day to demand trans and nonbinary rights reform! #DownWithPanoptica #DownWithFPNG

Ryan marked the trending hashtags and continued incorporating them into his own messages. Dakota, from the ill-fated support group, pulled at his jacketed elbow as he was in the middle of composing another tweet.

"What's up?"

Dakota gasped in the process of trying to get the whole message out in one breath, "My friend Mattie just texted me to tune into 95.7 FM, the university's radio. We're ready."

This is it, he thought. "Ok, got it. Now what?"

Dakota shrugged. "They're trying to circulate the announcement. Can someone pull up the radio on their phone or does someone have a boombox or speaker or something?"

"I've got a laptop," someone behind Ryan shouted. "Just got out of class. Whatcha need it for?"

"Is there any way to hook it up and project out of those speakers at the front of the plaza so we can all hear the broadcast?"

"What broadcast?"

"You'll see. If we can figure it out, that is," Dakota said.

"I can certainly try," they said. Ryan grabbed the stranger's hand – it turns out her name was Jay – and dragged her toward the front of the swarming crowd.

***

Alex tapped the radio studio's mic a few times, though they knew full well it was on, ready to go. They looked up to see the others, their headset blocking their ears from any outside noise. Through the thick pane of glass that separated Alex in the studio from their friends and Kieran, they all gave Alex a thumbs up.

***

At Springfield City Hall, Alex's taps transfigured into vibrant pounds in the ears of the masses as the speakers crackled into life. Alex's voice stole Ryan's breath as he realized who was speaking.

***

Alex let the post-tap silence drag on for a second or two before commencing their announcement, coughing their relatively unused voice to life.

"This is an emergency broadcast. Many of you don't know who I am, so let me start by introducing myself: my name is Alex Cesario. Some of you know me by the name 'Alexandra.' I am a nonbinary, genderfluid, transmasculine person from Springfield." They paused, unsure of how to continue. As people tuned into their frequency in waves, hopefully carried by the buzz on Twitter, Facebook, and all social media outlets, Alex imagined they'd have to repeat the message a few times. "My identity is *not* open to interpretation for strangers or the FPNG, and neither is yours. I'm, uh… I'm here to tell you that the Northeast Panoptic, owned by the Foundation for the Protection of Normative Gender, otherwise known as the Foundation or FPNG, has fallen.

"Earlier this fall, I was arrested at the airport for my gender presentation and taken to the Panoptic for rehabilitation. I repeat, the Northeast Panoptic has fallen. After we overthrew the FPNG's villainous prison, I escaped with the help of my friends and comrades, and have been in hiding until this very moment. I'm here to tell you that we've loosened the tight hold the Foundation holds over nonbinary, gender nonconforming, and gender variant people. Most of us are alive and well and we need you, supporters and allies, to spread the good word.

"I repeat, my name is Alex. If you're listening in now, I'm telling you that the Northeast Panoptic has fallen. The Foundation will surely try to tell you otherwise, but we can prove it—our freedom, our prison uniforms. Our supporters are gathering at Springfield City Hall as I speak…"

On and on Alex spoke, and each time they repeated, "The Northeast Panoptic has fallen," the more their confidence picked up steam and the more they believed, finally, that their coup had delivered a major blow to the Foundation. The repetition was a mantra, fortifying them with resilience and finally helping them believe in the success of their feat.

Alex looked up between the third and fourth iterations of their announcement and saw Kieran wildly pointing at their phone, which was facing outward so Alex could see the screen: it looked like some sort of news coverage on Facebook Live, with likes, loves, wows, and angry reacts flying across Kieran's screen. They paused and held up their hands to mime, "What's that?"

Mattie pushed Kieran out of the way and rolled their right index finger over and over, signifying that Alex should wrap up. They resumed, "The Northeast Panoptic, owned by the Foundation for the Protection of Normative Gender, otherwise known as the Foundation or FPNG, has fallen. I'm here to tell you that earlier this fall, I was arrested at the airport for my gender presentation and taken to the Panoptic for rehabilitation. I repeat, the Northeast Panoptic has fallen. Meet us at City Hall to join the fight. That concludes this broadcast." They placed the huge headphones down and ran out of the studio and around to the control room.

Alex said, "What were you saying?"

Kieran shoved their phone in Alex's face. "We're on the news!"

"Already?"

Kieran scoffed, "What, did you think that thousands of people converging in the city's center, the very axis of governmental control, would go unnoticed?"

Sure enough, Kieran's phone told Alex that their local TV station was in the midst of broadcasting a speculative emergency news announcement. "It seems that thousands of citizens have gathered at Springfield City Hall, carrying signs that read, "Down with the Foundation," and "Eliminate the FPNG." We're still investigating, but Alice Camper is in the field, interviewing the protesters."

The field reporter placed a finger to her earbud and nodded along with the anchor as he spoke. "Okay, okay," they said to themselves, and then addressed the camera, "Breaking news, according to those gathered at Springfield City Hall – I can't believe I'm saying this – the Northeast Regional Panoptic has fallen. The Panoptic's location is largely unknown to the general public, however we've contacted the Foundation for an official statement. Stay tuned as we continue to report from the front lines, where the protest and a radio broadcast from the University of Springfield is going viral. We'll get you that recording after the commercial break."

Alex's face flushed. "Holy shit. We did it."

"Now off to the city center! After that report, the Foundation will be looking for us here, no doubt," said Kieran. Mattie ushered the group out of the studio, who sprinted down the hall and out the back door.

The small group linked arms and waded downstream to City Hall, where Alex whipped out their temporary burner phone and called Ryan to ascertain his current location, who shouted, "By the speakers!" Alex then realized that over the shouting, yelling, cheering, and chanting, their broadcast was being played over City Hall's outside speakers in a continuous loop.

Soon, Alex locked eyes with Ryan in the same way they had with Kieran back during the fall of the Panoptic. All else faded into Alex's periphery and they pushed people aside and tackled their best friend, refusing to let each other go for a full minute.

I'm home, Alex thought.

"Holy crap, I missed you."

"Same here, Ryan." Alex tried to choke back the tears of relief that brimmed at the back of their eyes as their throat started to close, and then said, "Look who I brought with me," sweeping back their arm to reveal Juneau, who had been sprinting behind them like a shadow. Alex stepped aside to give them some space. Ryan and Juneau inched toward one another with tentative footfalls.

"Ryan, I…"

"You don't have to explain anything. I know what you had to do."

"It still doesn't excuse… What you must think of me."

"I think the world of you. I'm so proud of you, Juneau," he said without hesitation. They flung themselves into a passionate embrace that rivaled any Alex had ever seen.

Tears flooded Juneau and Ryan's eyes in such a way that brought Alex close to tears, too, moved by their endless affection for one another.

"It's been way too long, my love," Ryan said as he kissed Juneau passionately, and Alex turned to give the couple's reunion some privacy.

Roaring was all Alex could hear now, the elevated pitch deafening all else, like the post-concert hum they'd experienced several times as a teenager returning from seeing Disturbed and Slipknot. That raging thrum of white noise expanded like insulation foam and seeped into every crack and corner of Alex's ears.

What mattered then wasn't the ability to hear or Alex having full agency over all their senses. What mattered more than anything at that moment was the reality that their multimedia assault hadn't yet been stopped, and more importantly, it was working. *Take it in, Alex. Experience this moment. We've done it.*

Alex didn't have the slightest chance to sense Officer Paine lumbering toward them through the bustling, surging, screaming crowd. They turned just in time to see Paine's sickening smile before he covered their head with a dark, heavy sack. The surprise of his appearance and the blow Paine dealt to their sternum sucked the breath out of them in such a way that made them sure they would pass out on the spot before they even hit the pavement.

Before their body hit the ground, Alex heard Kieran's strong voice beside them shout, "WE ARE VALID."

After Alex's hip crushed into the pavement, Paine's voice cut through all else, even the deafening crowd around them. "I knew I'd find one of you, you little shit."

Alex bucked their body and attempted to butt their head into Paine, but he only pushed them back to the ground. Where was everyone? Where was Kieran? Would Kieran even hear their screams in this chaos?

Didn't anyone notice them down there, suffocating under the weight of Paine's hulking body and the Foundation once more, even in this moment of triumph?

Paine's spitting hisses cut even further into Alex, like knives in their ear, one bleeding cut ripping after the next with every word. "Even in this ridiculous getup, I recognized you right away, Cesario. I remember you from intake. My commanding officer at the Foundation sent me here, to Springfield, right after the fall of the Panoptic. They anticipated something like this. You couldn't just take your victory and quit there, could you? Was freedom not good enough? You think you're free, but just wait until…"

Alex started screaming bloody murder, aiming to shout as long and loud as they could until their voice went hoarse. Surely, someone would eventually turn around and notice. Officer Paine gathered Alex in a bear hug to drag them away.

Click.

Alex's self-defense training kicked in like a key sliding neatly into its lock; they'd been in this exact situation before, several times in fact, during a few Tang Soo Do self-defense classes they'd attended with Juneau at her dojang.

Click.

Bear hug. *You know what to do.*

Draw all your weight down.

Stomp, one foot.

Stomp, the other.

Bear down, slide out one leg into a horse stance and shoot both hands straight out.

Alex couldn't see for the darkness of the satchel smothering their head, but they did feel Paine's weight shift off-balance. *Perfect.*

Elbow to the stomach.

Elbow to the groin.

Alex popped their hip out and rotated Officer Paine over their hip and onto the rough pavement, stomping on him to keep him down and out.

"Alex!"

Hearing still muffled from the sack, Alex couldn't tell who called their name. They ripped the stifling sack from their head. A burst of cold air rushed at Alex and immediately cleared the stuffed feeling in their head. They blinked hard several times into the blinding light until their fuzzy vision picked up Kieran in front of them, a horrified look on their face. They saw Paine on the ground, restrained by both Juneau and Ryan.

Alex rubbed their head, trying to fully clear it.

"Alex, oh my God. Are you okay?" Kieran wrapped Alex in a tight embrace and held them steady.

"Paine can take his gender normative bullshit and shove it," Alex replied with a weak smile.

QUESTIONS FOR CLASS AND BOOK CLUB DISCUSSIONS

1. What are some common attributes (physical or otherwise) that you associate with being "masculine" or "male?" Why? Name several characteristics that challenge those stereotypes.
2. What are some common attributes that you associate with being "feminine" or "female?" Why? Name several characteristics that challenge those stereotypes.
3. What characteristics do you associate with nonbinary or gender nonconforming identities? Why, and from where do these characteristics originate (e.g. your own presumptions, media, etc.)?
4. Discuss the differences between biological sex, gender, gender presentation, and gender identity.
5. How do binary identities differ from nonbinary and gender nonconforming identities? Explain.
6. How do nonbinary identities fit within, interrogate, and/or subvert any gender theories with which you are familiar?
7. Do you recognize any nonbinary people or fictional characters in books or media? If so, who? How would you characterize the representation of these nonbinary or GNC characters?
8. Explain and discuss how specific policies, microaggressions, and/or social norms discriminate against trans, nonbinary, and gender nonconforming people. Examples can be found in education, religion, healthcare, and public accommodations.
9. Provide examples of policies, laws, and measures that *protect* nonbinary and gender nonconforming people.

APPENDIX: GENDER TERMINOLOGY
REFERENCE CHART[1]

Agender   Individual who feels they have no gender identity, or who identifies not as male or female but 'neutral'

Bigender   Individual who sees themselves as having two gender identities. The separate genders could be male, or female, mixed, or other, and may exist at the same time or entirely distinctly and separately from the other gender

Cisgender   Individual who identifies with the gender they were assigned at birth

Genderfluid   Individual for whom gender is unfixed; they fluctuate between different gender identities, one of which may or may not include their assigned gender at birth. These gender identities may be binary, nonbinary, both, neither, or fluctuate, and may all exist at the same time or separately

Genderqueer   Individual who does not subscribe to conventional gender distinctions but identifies with neither, both, or a combination of male and female genders. Genderqueer is often used as an umbrella term referring to gender identities that do not fit into the socially constructed binary gender norms

Hormone Replacement Therapy (HRT)   A procedure in which the body's natural hormones are replaced or boosted by medical means, such as with pills or injections. For someone assigned female at birth, this might mean taking testosterone to replace the estrogen in their body, or vice versa for someone assigned male at birth

---

[1] Not meant to be comprehensive; these gender terms are subject to change based on the individual.

LGBTQIA	Acronym that stands for: Lesbian, Gay, Bisexual, Transgender, Queer, Intersex, Asexual
MOGAI	Acronym that stands for: Marginalized Orientations, Gender Identities, and Intersex. This acronym is often used to be more inclusive than LGBTQIA
Nonbinary	Individual who does not identify with traditional binary gender identities
Nonbinary transgender	Individual whose gender identity is different from the gender they were assigned at birth, and whose identity is not traditionally of a binary gender (see: *Nonbinary*)
Transgender	Individual whose gender identity is different from the gender they were assigned at birth

ABOUT THE AUTHOR

Shalen Lowell (they/them) is a transgender and genderfluid author, blogger, and poet originally from Woburn, Massachusetts, who now resides in Southern Maine. They specialize in fiction that represents the intersection of fantasy and postmodern genres and queer literature, with particular emphasis on illustrating, highlighting, and validating the lives, struggles, and experiences of nonbinary and gender nonconforming LGBTQ+ folx. Shalen has also contributed several personal essays and chapters on trans/genderfluid identity and expression and binary privilege to edited volumes such as *Privilege Through the Looking-Glass*; *Massachusetts' Best Emerging Poets*; *Challenging Genders: Nonbinary Experiences of Those Assigned Female at Birth*; *Expanding the Rainbow: Exploring the Relationships of Bi+, Trans, Ace, Polyam, Kink, and Intersex People*; and *Scientists and Poets #RESIST*. *Gender Optics* is their first published novel.

Made in the USA
Middletown, DE
13 December 2020